Onwards & Upwards

Paul Askew

First Published 2017
By Relish Publications
Morpeth
Northumberland, NE61 1PY.

ISBN: 978-0-9934678-5-1

Author - Paul Askew
Publisher – Duncan Peters
Project Manager, Photographer, Editor – Andy Richardson
Creative Director – Matt Eld
Production Director – Paul Naylor
Editor At Large – Victoria Copley
Art Director and Additional Photography – Michelle Martin

Printed in Poland on behalf of Latitude Press

To all the young chefs, waiters and sommeliers who have dreams, standards, a work ethic, creativity and passion. Never, never give up. Always onwards and upwards.

To my lovely family: wife Helen and son Harry, for being so loving and supportive.

To my late parents: Marjorie 'Moriarty' Askew and Captain 'Barnacle' Bill Askew, who prepared me with their eccentric genius for the journey of life.

And to my three great sisters Anne, Susan and Jane.

Preface

Onwards and Upwards. It seemed like a fitting title. It's the phrase that staff, friends and family have grown accustomed to and it's also been the story of my life. Onwards and upwards. It sort-of fits.

I've been asked over many years when my first book would be out. And I've told friends and guests that I'm not quite ready, that the time is not quite right. So what's changed? Well, in some ways, everything has.

On a professional level, I've started to realise the dreams I had when I began cooking professionally. Back then, I wanted to create my own style, to follow the classic lineage that began with the Roux brothers contribution to the UK dining scene.

My vision was to respect great produce, to cook with integrity, to follow the seasons and to present my food with flair. I wanted to do that in a restaurant that bore the hallmarks of my own, individual style. At The Art School, in Liverpool, that's precisely what I'm doing.

Having earned my spurs, worked with others, learned valuable lessons and put them into good practice, the time came to go it alone here in my home city.

And in recent years, we've gone from strength to strength as The Art School has embodied my idea of being a place for the Culinary Arts.

We're creating the best food of my career, we're continually striving to improve standards and we're also placing an enormous focus on service, making sure people enjoy a warm welcome with plenty of Liverpudlian charm.

On a personal level, there has been quantum change.

My beloved mother, Marjorie, passed away quite recently, leaving a profound sense of loss.

Cooking for my guests brought succour. I poured myself into my work like never before. I was – and remain – determined to honour her memory, committed to giving my guests the very best of me and unwilling to waiver.

One of the dishes in this book pays tribute to her and it featured on BBC TV's Great British Menu. I hope some of you will cook it – I hope all of you will enjoy it.

My son, Harry, is also approaching the age that I was when I started to cut loose and dream big.

And so I wanted to share with him some of the stories of my travels and adventures.

Family has always been enormously important to me.

My father's work meant I'd travelled the world by the time I'd left school.

The flavours of my travels have profoundly influenced my cooking. But the importance of family influences more than just food. It also shapes the way we go about our work here at The Art School.

We put the wants and needs of our guests first - always. We work hard with our staff to make sure they feel valued and respected. And we also try to make our staff feel valued and welcome.

We want them to feel as though they're returning to their home-from-home, as though they're part of The Art School's extended family.

I recall reading a piece from a Roux brothers book, about being In The Kitchen.

It spoke of treating all workers with the same consideration, remaining calm and composed in a crisis, seeking excellence and sharing culinary techniques and theories with younger members of staff.

It described a great chef as being like the conductor of a great orchestra: seeking respect, love and affection. The Roux brothers changed the game.

They introduced respect and standards to the kitchen and we uphold the principles that they espoused.

I'm delighted to welcome you into my life, to share my stories and my recipes.

And I'm delighted to present my debut book to you.

We look forward to welcoming you to The Art School. We're grateful that you've joined us for the ride.

My life has ever been Onwards and Upwards, and as I continue to develop, that remains true to this day.

Paul Askew

October 2017

Forewords

I have known Paul for over 20 years. We first met when he was at The Philarmonic, in Liverpool. I really discovered what he was all about when he became Chef-Patron, London Carriage Works.

During Paul's tenure I fell in love twice. Firstly with the hotel and building and secondly with Paul's cooking. What became apparent during that era was Paul's complete love of kitchens, cooking and food. However, even more profound was his total passion for the produce he sources from exceptional suppliers.

Whenever I am in his company or simply talking with him I'm staggered by his total – and I mean TOTAL – vision of the produce he wishes to use and cook with. There's Andrew Pimbley from Claremont Farm for garden produce; Simon and Nigel Buckmaster at Wards Fish; Callum Edge for his butchery and Peter Jones at Wirral Watercress, to name but a few.

Onwards and Upwards is the second part of Paul's dream. The first was opening his exquisite Art School restaurant in Liverpool. Paul wanted to cook in his own place, to popularise

fine dining for Liverpool and to win accolades. The second was to spread the message about what he does and about his passion for great produce, which is precisely what Onwards and Upwards does.

I am truly honoured to have been asked to write a foreword for Paul's first book. Paul is a very dear friend, a fellow cook and a Fellow of The Royal Academy of Culinary Arts. He is a consummate professional.

I feel very confident that the true depth of Paul's passion and commitment will come through in this gorgeous cookery book and I hope that you all enjoy it as much as I have. Paul is a true food champion of the North West, Liverpool and Beyond.

Steven Doherty

Steven Doherty is a Master of Culinary Arts. He was the first Englishman to hold and run a three Michelin Star restaurant, at Le Gavroche.

Paul is a true Liverpudlian talent. He is Liverpool through and through with a heart as big as the city itself.

Paul cooks his own style of Modern British food, working with the seasons of the North and only using the best ingredients.

He has truly created a very special restaurant in The Art School.

It is full of passion and guile and Paul cooks in a modest but very engaging way.

With his young and talented staff, Paul has created a true culinary landmark.

In time, it will surely get the recognition it deserves.

This book gives an insight into the total dedication of Paul and his staff as they go on a culinary journey in search of only the best.

I salute you Paul. You deserve everything that will surely come your way.

Nigel Haworth

Nigel Haworth, not only showcases his own gastronomic brilliance at Northcote, but sets the benchmark for fine dining across the UK. Nigel is now approaching his 30th anniversary at Northcote displaying an instinctive understanding of his region and a cultivated awareness for diners' needs.

Contents

10 My story

32 How to make a dish

36 Producers

38 Two Cathedrals Honey

40 Wirral Water Cress

42 Wards Fishmongers

48 Senna Lane Farm

54 The Rhug Estate

62 Claremont Farm

68 Edge & Son

70 Recipes

72 Spring

Starters

74 Warm Salad of Honey-glazed Roasted Fig, Spring Leaves & Tymsboro Goat's Cheese

76 Fillet of Menai Mackerel, Blood Orange Dressing & Herb Infused Goats Curd

78 North Sea Haddock with Brown Shrimp & Herb Crust, Pickled Cucumber & Mustard

Mains

82 Breast of Goosnargh Duckling served with Rhubarb & Orange Puree

86 Confit Leg & Breast of Organic Rhug Estate Chicken & Claremont Farm Asparagus

90 A Plate of Callum's Oldfield Farm Galloway Beef to include Tongue, Cheek & Sirloin

Desserts

94 Valhrona Dark Chocolate Bordelou, Mango Foam, Matcha Green Tea Sorbet & Cremeux

96 The Captain's Trophy

100 Crème Brûlée

104 Summer

Starters

106 Cornish Red Mullet with Lemon, Parsley & Brown Shrimp Risotto and Pastis Sauce

110 Fillet of Cured Wild Sea Trout with Sea Herbs, Samphire & Pickled Cucumber

112 Roast Courgettes with Curthwaite Goat's Curd & Tempura Courgette Flower

Mains

114 Summer Memories with Marjorie

118 Peterhead Turbot served with Native Lobster, Lime and Mango salad and Mousseline potatoes

122 Pan-roast Fillet of Peterhead Hake, served with Pomme Mousseline & Southport Potted Shrimp

124 Asian Marinated Tofu, Spaghetti Vegetables, Baby Spinach, Girolle Mushrooms & Pak Choi Shoots

Desserts

128 Passion Fruit Delice

130 Lime Tart

134 Coconut Ice Cream with a Chickpea Meringue, Rum Roasted Pineapple & Pineapple Gel

136 Autumn

Starters

138 Warm Salad of Herdwick Lamb's Tongue, Butcher's Wife Black Pudding & Autumn Leaves

140	Confit of Autumn Rabbit Pie with Pickled Vegetables & Piccalilli Vinaigrette
144	Fillet of Turbot with Cucumber Tagliatelle, Palourde Clams, Cockles & Keta Caviar
148	Breast of Red Leg Partridge served with Puy Lentils, Smoked Southport Pork Loin, Leeks & Pear

Mains

150	Veal Cutlet, Shin and Marrow Bone with Girolles, Parsley Root & Heritage Carrots
152	Liverpool Bay Seabass, Sauce of Palourde Clams & Celeriac Puree served with Rainbow Chard
156	Pan-roast Fillet of Peterhead Hake with a Risotto of Filey Crab

Desserts

158	Guanaja Dark Chocolate Mille Feuille
162	Ormskirk Damson Sorbet with Granny Smith Apples, White Chocolate Soil
164	Pavlova of Gin-soaked Blackberries, Turkish Delight Ice Cream & White Chocolate Soil

166	Winter

Starters

168	Seared King Scallop with Butcher's Wife Black Pudding & Romanesco Cous Cous
172	Baked Salsify, Parmesan Crust, Roast Navet, Parsnip Puree, Leaves & Sour Cherry Dressing
174	Senna Lane Farm Pork Belly, Cheek plus Southport Smoked Loin & Edges Butcher's Wife Black Pudding
176	Twice Baked Soufflé of Local Pink Tip Spinach & Mrs Kirkham's Lancashire Cheese

Mains

178	Mr Ward's Loin of "Red Deer" Venison served with Girolles, Black Truffle & Cavolo Nero
182	Pave Rump of Dry Aged Lakeland Beef
186	Roast Breast of Squab Pigeon with Beetroot Puree & Foie Gras

Winter Desserts

190	Granny Smith Apple and Calvados Sponge with a Vanilla Mascarpone & Candied Walnuts
192	Sharing Plate, Includes: Pistachio Macaron, Chocolate Tart, Orange Delice & Choux Bun
198	The Art School Cellars
204	Glossary - Bread
206	Glossary - Stocks
208	Glosary - Seasoning
212	Glossary - Puree
214	Glossary - Basics
216	Glossary of Terminology, Caveats, Substitutes and How To Use This Book
222	Index
224	Credits and Thank Yous

My story

Food has always been a major part of my life. It was from year dot, from the time that I was just a child. I started life in the North East – Sunderland to be precise – and food has been an ever-present feature ever since.

Our family left when I was four-and-a-half because my father's work took him around the world. He was in shipping and we called him Barnacle Bill. He was a wandering nomad of the seas. I led a peripatetic childhood, moving from here to there all the time. We started in Sunderland, then moved to Liverpool, then moved to London, then came back to Liverpool. At the age of 11, I was shipped off to Dubai.

My father worked for Blue Star Line, which was the shipping division of the Vesty Group, sailing container ships around the world. He was a Master Mariner, Captain of the ship. He'd ship New Zealand lamb, American apples, Argentinian beef – you name it. It's ironic that I'm the guy who's doing the exact opposite; I'm encouraging people to buy local, to use their farm shop, to cook with what's in season.

Bill was at sea for 40 odd years and then at the end of his career he came ashore to work as an Operations Director. His job was to fill the ships with cargo, crew them, and send them around the world.

My father was the reason for me going to Dubai. His job was to establish a container port on behalf of Blue Star Line and I left the UK to go with my parents, while my two sisters stayed home. It was a huge change – I'd never been on an aeroplane before. I was starting a new schooling system and living in a totally different environment.

I think my mum put me on a plane with a sign on my lapel, you know, like Paddington Bear. It probably said something like: 'Please look after this child, he eats chips'. And then from the moment I stepped on the plane, I took it off and pretended I was a travelling businessman, you know, like 007.

That era was exciting and daunting at the same time. I'd done a year at the local Grammar School, on the Wirral, in Liverpool, and the next thing I knew I was bound for Dubai to start in the Baccalaureate system, which was French.

My school in Dubai was like the United Nations. Straight away, I was mixing with different cultures where there were different foods and different views. Food featured heavily and I remember going to a fish market and going fishing off a dhow. Those experiences were mind-boggling and in my mind's eye those things are as clear as day. I enjoyed being exposed to good quality food. I was as obsessed about food as I was about heroes like Jacques Cousteau. With fish, for instance, I was transfixed about the market and about the way things were cooked. The fish were unlike anything I'd ever seen, they were incredible.

It was literally like Star Wars meets the fish market. It was the same with the fruit and vegetable market, where I saw the most unusual produce. And so, as a young man, I became quite obsessed by it all.

Travelling from such an early age also taught me about human behaviour. If I add it all up, I had eight different schools and 14 different homes in my first 18 years.

I was virtually living on my own by the time I left school. It wasn't a case of me leaving my parents, it was more like my parents leaving me.

The thing is, when you move so often, you learn very quickly about first impressions and going with your gut instinct. You have to, because otherwise life can teach you some very, very harsh lessons.

Back then, I used to think it was terrible that I'd just made a new set of friends and then I'd be dashing off again, like the travelling gypsy caravan.

At the time, I hated what was going on. Yet I also loved the travel, I loved seeing those places. And looking back now, it was probably the making of me.

I feel very comfortable and without wishing to sound arrogant, I'm usually a pretty good judge of character. That's because of those formative years.

My father probably did me a huge favour, even though I didn't think that at the time and I just wanted to stay in one place.

I met people from all around the world and one of my best mates at school came from a very, very wealthy Arab family, of Palestinian origin. They'd left Palestine because of the troubles.

On one occasion, he invited me to his house for tea. I imagined we'd just be going to a normal house to eat a few butties. When I got there, it had its own mosque and its own driveway.

We were picked up from school by a chauffeur driven Mercedes and when we got back to his there was a track around the property with motorbikes on it. I'd thought we'd just be going back to his house for a bit of a giggle but it was like being invited to tea with a royal family.

On another occasion, we were out in the desert flying falcons. There were insane experiences that even in your wildest imagination you wouldn't consider.

I remember thinking: 'is this really happening?'

Paul Askew

On my 13th birthday, I held a party. I asked one of the guys to help with the food and he turned up with all of the ingredients to make a biryani. To be honest, I probably had more fun making the biryani than I did with the party.

Apart from English and American students, I found myself with Palestinians, Iraqis, Iranians, Belgians, French, Germans and kids from all over the world.

At a very early age, I became quite worldly wise. I had to, just to survive. I was surrounded by all points of view and found it fascinating how different people were just because of their country of origin.

I learned that things are rarely simple; there are usually complicated reasons for troubles in different parts of the world. The whole experience gave me a measured understanding.

I did a lot of listening and learned not to engage my mouth until I knew what I was responding to. It put me in good stead.

Mixing with different cultures made my gastronomic life more interesting than it might otherwise have been. I distinctly remember the first dish that I ever made: chicken biryani. I learned it from one of the boys who was associated with the school, in Dubai.

Our living quarters were arranged as a quadrangle, with a pool at the centre, and nearly all of the British and American boys were together.

Most of our fathers were in shipping and there were guys who'd come in to clean the pools or make up the rooms. They were always helpful and if ever there were any other little jobs – cooking or cleaning – they'd help out.

On my 13th birthday, I held a party. I asked one of the guys to help with the food and he turned up with all of the ingredients to make a biryani. To be honest, I probably had more fun making the biryani than I did with the party.

That might have had something to do with the brilliant food – and it might have been because of my unrequited love for a particular girl that I was pursuing.

The guy taught me the method and biryani remains one of the simplest and tastiest dishes that I cook at home.

On other occasions, there'd be trips to the spice market, where everything would be fresh and would be weighed out in piles. There'd be regular trips to the fruit and vegetable markets too.

Food became a fascination.

I think that all stems back to my earliest memories, back in Sunderland. I distinctly remember my grandmother being a brilliant home cook.

The minute she finished breakfast she was making lunch, the minute she finished lunch she was making afternoon tea, the minute she finished afternoon tea she was making dinner.

Her name was Sarah Askew, though by birth she was a McCutcheon, a Northern Irish Methodist. Nobody messed with her, she was incredible.

She was intrinsically connected to food. The kettle was never off and the kitchen was never empty. It was constant.

She'd be there sharpening the carving knife on the back step so often that the step had a big groove in it by the end of it and the knife was as sharp as a razor.

Everything was made, from the cakes and scones and pies to the mains. It was all done from scratch.

My mum was also a good cook. She focused on simple food but she had some signature dishes too. There was never anything fancy but she was capable of really good cooking. She loved markets, too, not just food markets but any kind.

She loved having a rummage round and I think I inherited that from her. I can spend hours just rummaging round to find the right stuff. In many ways, I still do. Every day we'll be on the line to the suppliers, finding out what's good.

And I still get just as much of a kick out of dealing with those guys as I used to. This morning, for instance, I was at Wirral Watercress, picking oyster leaf, the wild garlic and apple marigold. It's fantastic.

To me, that's what inspires true chefs. It's all about great produce that's in peak condition. If you're not inspired by the ingredients you need to pack up. It shouldn't be about anything else.

That's my belief in food. If you start off with ingredients of extremely high integrity and flavour and you can do something that's sympathetic to them then you're on the right track. It's when you try and mess with them too much that you lose people.

For me, it's very much an art, rather than a science. There is some science in what we do, of course, particularly in pastry. But artistry is key: hence The Royal Academy of Culinary Arts, not The Royal Academy of Culinary Science. There's a subtle difference in that.

Most people would say that on the larder sections, main course sections and garnish, you need to become very instinctive and proactive. The ingredients are different each day.

14

What might require 5 grams one day could easily require 8 grams the next day. What might take 12 minutes to cook one day might easily require 15 minutes the next.

That's why we encourage butchery and fishmongery here and doing everything from scratch. Until you get intertwined with the ingredients, you don't even know whether it should be sous vide or pan fried.

These days, people learn how to water bath something at 52 degrees for two days before they learn how to take a lamb saddle off the bone. I just don't get that. We need to learn classical methods first and understand our ingredients before we decide to cook in that way, not the other way around.

Why would you do that with a prime cut? That's where it loses me. It does a great disservice to young chefs.

But I've strayed off the subject and I wanted to tell you more about my time on the road and how that shaped the way I cook today.

So let's head back to Dubai. Another of the beauties of my father's job was that he'd fly me to different corners of the world. He knew the opportunity was there and he wanted me to make the most of it.

He'd learnt the value of travel by spending so many years on the road.

He took me to India for a couple of weeks so that I could see how different things were and how valuable life was.

I think he wanted to show me how lucky I was to have quite a privileged upbringing.

I loved India. It is just the most colourful, incredible place on the planet. It's bonkers.

The food is fantastic despite the ever-present issues and problems. Visiting at such an early age gave me a better sense of perspective.

My father wasn't always easy, but he was wise. There were times when he could be Sgt Major-ish – and during my teens I fought against him and rebelled. Looking back, it all makes sense now. I can see how he was trying to help.

After Dubai, my father moved to Singapore and he spent the last decade or so as the Managing Director of Austasia Line and Merillion Shipping, both subsidiaries of Blue Star Line.

He worked at a high level and that came with lots of privileges.

Part of his job was entertaining the crew and the captain of his ships when they came into port.

His hospitality was legendary, a bit like my approach to partying. The way he'd host people was off the scale and my mum was the same; she'd be on the piano singing while dad was handing out the whiskies.

It was hilarious. One minute you have this old sailor in the corner with a squeeze box and then his wife would be singing and dancing. There was beer and unlimited food. The hospitality of my father was memorable; it was his work but he absolutely adored it.

Even family gatherings were like that. It all revolved around food and a good shindig. I loved that. For me, one of life's true pleasures is sharing great food, great drink and great company.

For me, they are all about conviviality. You know, the great food should come as a given, as should great wine and great service.

We are there to ensure our guests at the table have a great time, not the other way around. I think it's a great shame that people over the years in our business have made themselves more important than the guests and I don't believe in that. True hospitality is selfless, warm and fun as well as being technically correct.

We are there to facilitate our guests to have the best, best time. I've experienced that myself when I've been to a great restaurant and I've literally cried with joy. My hope is that we can do that for people as well, in our way. We want to look through the kitchen window into the restaurant and see smiling faces and animation among our guests.

As we all know, the word restaurant originates from a sense of restoring people and making them stronger. From a nutritional point of view that's obvious, but it's also to restore them from tiredness; it's almost an holistic interpretation. A great meal is good for the soul, I always say. When you have a great meal with great wine and great company, it's good for the soul. We all adore that, don't we? There's not many people I know who wouldn't be interested in that.

Apart from the arty side of food, I think I get my job satisfaction from seeing very, very happy people having memorable times and wanting to come back again. That's what chefs get a kick out of.

My father stayed in Singapore until he was 65. And I travelled a fair bit more before leaving school. Eventually, I returned to the UK on a permanent basis for school then I'd travel to see my father every summer, Christmas and Easter.

We are there to ensure our guests at the table have a great time, not the other way around. I think it's a great shame that people over the years in our business have made themselves more important than the guests and I don't believe in that. True hospitality is selfless, warm and fun as well as being technically correct.

I'd be off exploring every time there was a holiday.

Singapore was incredible. For me, Singapore is an even bigger centre of culinary excellence and diversity than Dubai.

There's great Chinese food, Malaysian food, Indian food, Colonial food and dishes from the Pacific Rim. It's all there.

There's great produce, fish markets, unique flavours and mind-blowing smells from the hawker centres. That time was incredible. I remember a 10-year-old guy on the side of the pavement, wafting his fan to get the charcoal going to the right temperature so that he could cook the chicken satay.

To this day, that street food is still some of the best I've ever tasted. That little guy probably didn't know how to cook anything else but he was just brilliant at cooking satay.

Those memories stay with me. I recall my dad fishing a crab from a tank and the chefs cooking chilli crab in front of him.

Again, for them, freshness was everything. The Singaporeans were literally pulling fish, crabs, lobster, frogs and turtles out of the tank and cooking it to order.

I think because it was such a hot and humid climate, they were cautious about food hygiene. So everything was really fresh with these wonderful seasonings; ginger, chilli, garlic, lemongrass. It was just delicious.

I was excited by flavours as a kid. In Singapore, we were fortunate in that a maid used to come in and look after the house. She'd show me how to cook, even simple dishes like fried rice. It was incredible to learn like that – and I was only 14.

Within a year, I was working in a kitchen. I took my first job at Thornton Hall, on the Wirral, as a kitchen porter.

My father didn't mind me working in kitchens while I was at school but he didn't think I would specialise in it.

Later, when he realised I wanted to become a chef, there was a sense of "you're not going to work downstairs in the galley boy!".

To him, to work in the galley was the last chance saloon. He didn't get it. He didn't understand cheffing. He didn't connect that you could have greatness, that there were men like Albert Roux. He didn't appreciate that, whereas I did.

I knew where I wanted to go. To me, in his own way, my father was a chef, though his title was 'captain'., just as his father was a chief engineer, a master mariner.

In many ways, I'm also a captain. I'm a chef de cuisine. My father was sailing container ships around the world but my ship is in here, in the kitchen. My crew is my brigade.

One of my favourite analogies is football and rugby. A kitchen of chefs is similar to a team of footballers or rugby players. You've all got your jobs to do and you have to work for each other, there has to be co-ordination and timing. For the captain, or head chef, it's about who's playing and who's on the bench - or indeed who gets dropped? Who needs training?

My father was a huge influence and one of my biggest regrets is that he didn't get to see The Art School or The London Carriage Works, though he did see me at The Philharmonic Hall, in Liverpool.

My father passed away at 66. We only had 12 months of him back in the UK, after retirement. The whole point was that as a family we would finally all be back in one place.

Unfortunately he was diagnosed with lung cancer and passed away after three or four months, so we lost that opportunity. My mum was on her own for a long time after that, until she passed recently too.

But what my father gave us in a roundabout way was priceless . I definitely benefitted from the travel, the hospitality and the experiences we had. As a kid, I was living around the world and going on long haul flights every five minutes.

At Thornton Hall, I learned from a chef who'd been away on the cruise ships and was technically very accomplished. But our ideas about food were very different. I'd seen the world and had a more adventurous palate. His job was to deliver hotel food and he was incredibly good at it.

The environment back then was completely different to the kitchens of today. Back then, there'd be a few ladles or frying pans around the back of the head or a cleaver in the fridge door if somebody had upset someone else.

All those sorts of things happened. Though nobody could profess to enjoying that sort of rough and tumble, I did enjoy the banter and camaraderie. As a group, we got off on the hustle and bustle and the daily challenge of working in the kitchen.

Cooking is a lot like rugby. You know, it's five minutes to noon and look around: 'guys, are we ready for this?' And then the whistle blows and the checks start coming in.

Most chefs would say they enjoy the adrenalin rush and the daily challenge of dealing with that. It's not a grind, it comes with huge peaks and then it settles down, then we rest for a short while and then it goes again in the evening.

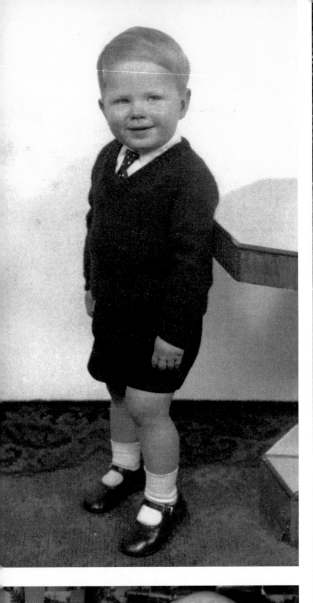

To this day, if I'm ever off on a Saturday, if I'm overseas on an annual holiday, for instance, I still feel strange when it's time for service and I'm not there. It's bizarre. But you think about it and feel like you should be doing it.

Camaraderie is great, but I'm no fan of shouting or getting worked up. The best brigades I've ever worked in have been virtually silent. People are going about their work and it's all about a nod and a look. Nobody has to shriek and shout and rant and rave.

I always say that if I have to rant and rave then there's something really serious because I'll not do that. If I can, my job is to absorb the pressure and allow them to perform.

I grew up in the kitchens where if you weren't getting shouted at there was something wrong. Even if you were doing things right you were getting shouted at.

For me, that's just white noise. It's a short-term game. You look at that approach and that style of management is dead and buried now.

It's not about that, especially in a northern city like Liverpool, where you have to grow your own brigade. It's not like London, where there's a glut of cooks. I can't call in an ex-Michelin star chef from here or there.

I'm building my own culture of service and of food production. You do that by building confidence and building people, not by the white noise, bullying approach. Eventually, people switch off. They're not going to stay there and work for you. I aspire to help and create, to lift and build, not to knock down.

Don't get me wrong, you'll sometimes get a very arrogant young man or young woman and then your job is to bring them into line, which I find much more difficult than nurturing people. It's quite interesting the way things evolve.

The people skills I developed as a young man have helped me now more than ever before.

My career progressed after those early stints as a kitchen porter. My father, however, didn't let me have things my own way. As ever, although we didn't see eye to eye at the time, there was method in his madness.

I'd done well in my O levels, passing nine without much work. I think I surprised everyone – including myself – because I wasn't really a very diligent academic type.

My father wanted me to stay on but he wasn't keen on me signing up for culinary college. He equated that with a job in the galley. So we had all these arguments.

He told me if I was serious about it and really wanted to do it then I'd have to do a management course, a hotel management course. He wanted me to do my A levels first, which I hated.

I carried on working at Thornton Hall then moved with my Sous Chef to another local restaurant called Pollard's Inn, which was a family-owned place on the Wirral.

It's owned by the breweries now but at the time it was owned by a fabulous eccentric called Jack Pollard, who wanted the best restaurant in the area.

The Sous Chef was an ex-Savoy guy who'd worked in Anton Mosimann's brigade.

He knew some good stuff and I felt I was moving forward with him so I stuck at it. Within no time, I was a Commis Chef, rather than a pot washer.

My A levels didn't go so well. I was playing a lot of rugby and working in the restaurant, so I didn't have much time for studying; I was more interested in booze-ups and hellraising.

I just wanted to have a bit of fun for two years.

When school was finally over, I went to Wirral Metropolitan College where I did a two-year hotel management qualification.

In his funny old way, my father did me a favour by sending me there because I had to do accountancy, service, housekeeping, HR and everything else.

Of course, I specialised in culinary art and I did extra tuition and learned how to do butter carvings and absorbed all of the French influences that were taught.

Back then, the Roux brothers were on the march. The book, New Classic Cuisine, had just come out and it revolutionised the way I saw food. As a chef, I had my love of great ingredients and a passion for honest cooking.

Inspired by my gran and from my travels; I had an aptitude for organisation, from my father; and I had a love of art, from my mother.

On reflection, I can see how the stars align, why I came to be the way I am. Mum was arty, whether at painting or gardening. She did a bit of watercolouring and was very creative.

My father was the bullish, businessman, who could be quite hard-nosed while also being very friendly, jolly and hospitable.

I'm building my own culture of service and of food production. You do that by building confidence and building people, not by the white noise, bullying approach. Eventually, people switch off. They're not going to stay there and work for you.

As I neared the end of my teens, Pollards was bought by Greenalls, which also owned De Vere Hotels.

The new broom saw some promise in me and offered me a training programme at Hale Barns, Altrincham, in South Manchester. I stayed for almost three years until I fell out of love with their style of food. They just wanted to do prawn cocktail, well done steak and black forest gateaux by the bucket load.

I was fascinated by nouvelle cuisine books and by Michel and Albert Roux. I wanted to create something new, something inspired by ingredients and my travels.

I just thought there had to be something better than that and to be fair the Head Chef at the time felt the same, he wanted to do some of his own dishes too.

Eventually, things came to a head and I had one of those stroppy, rebellious moments where I said if I couldn't put any of my own food on in the restaurant, I'd go.

They told me that the menus were dictated by Head Office and I'd got to get my head down and get on with it. So I left.

The question for me was simple: where to next?

I didn't particularly enjoy London. I'd lived there as a kid and then when I'd been at college I'd written without success to The Savoy, The Dorchester and The Ritz. I'd got nothing back from any of them. So I thought there was no way I was going back.

On reflection, it's clear the reason I didn't get those jobs was because I had a Merseyside postcode. There was a great deal of prejudice against Liverpool back then, which still grates.

It's changed now, of course, but it made me want to prove a point. It made me want to do well without having to be in London – and that flame still burns. There's nothing more satisfying than changing perceptions and showing people capital city standards in Liverpool.

My best mate at the time was based in New York. He was playing MLS soccer for the Albany Capitals. So I flew out to join him and we enjoyed the best of our bachelor years in upstate New York.

I got a job working in a restaurant for a lovely Jewish gentleman, Ernest Feldman, who owned restaurants downtown but also had a huge outside catering business. It meant that one minute I was literally a sous chef in a big brigade doing a 500-cover sit down for Sarratoga Race Track and the next day I was back in the van going to some lawyer's

house to do a table of 12 while they were snorting cocaine off the glass table in front of me. There's a kitchen confidential book there, believe me.

I was classically trained and had an English accent, so I was pushed to the front. The Americans adored anything to do with the Brits.

One minute I might be doing dressed lobster and a carved rack of lamb in a private house, then I'd be down at the restaurant in Albany working as a Relief Chef.

Like Dubai, I found myself in very-international surrounds. I was working with chefs from across the globe. So there was me and guys from Ireland, Bolivia and Bulgaria – from anywhere in the world. I was the chief whip, having to do what the Executive Chef wanted.

American restaurants these days can be utterly remarkable. The USA has some of the best chefs in the world. The provenance of ingredients and the way they respect them is off the scale. But back then, it was very different. They used to criticise British food but in many ways they were in a worst state.

I came back from New York about two years later. I'd been offered arranged marriages to extend my stay, but my Visa was up and it was time to come home.

Carl, my friend, had been offered a soccer coaching job, so he was off to do something else too. I felt like I couldn't go much further in Albany and I wanted to be back in Liverpool.

When I came home, I got offered head chef jobs immediately. I was 25 and though I took a promotion, it was too soon. To get a head chef position at that age was way, way too early. At that age, you think you can do it all. And from a culinary perspective, I was well-equipped. But from a management side, I was a long way short.

I had to manage a brigade, get a gross profit on each dish and manage the staff costs. I was dealing with things that were nothing to do with cooking and I wasn't ready. That's something I'm very aware of these days, when I work with colleges and young cooks. I have a real issue with colleges that they teach kids how to make the best food but they don't necessarily teach them how to make a profit from it.

And that causes huge conflict. Some of my worst arguments have been about ordering, when I've been told we need another 2% out of something or another 5% out of something else. It can sometimes cripple a dish. Chefs often find out those harsh realities when they're working, rather than at college, and it's often really damaging. I think those issues cripple a lot of chefs and that's why we lose so many.

I loved commissioning the artwork, Monsieur Mural, Matt Williams, and going to the auctions to get antiques that fit in every corner. And in a way, it's a bit like that with the food.
I search and search.

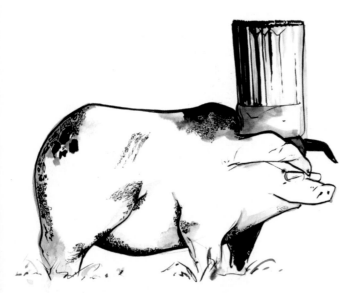

The brigades are shrinking so there's more work to do and less time to focus on the food. You almost have to employ a kitchen manager these days to get all of the elements done properly. You know, there's the environmental health, the stock take and the ordering, before you start to cook.

Here, I've got a great team who can take care of that. Thank God for the people I work with.

I was 24 or 25, then, when I took my first head chef job, which was at Wincham Hall, in Northwich. Although it no longer exists – it was turned back into a private residence – it was a lovely place and I spent three years there. Looking back, I tend to think people aren't ready to move into the head chef role until they're about 30, when they're more mature and have worked with decent quality people.

There were a few places after that, where things didn't come to fruition: it was the usual story of being promised the earth only to end up being short changed.

And then I came back to Liverpool. The Philharmonic Hall was having a £10 million refurbishment, from 1993 to 1995. They wanted someone to run a new restaurant, plus their backstage catering and corporate hospitality. The biggest thing was their summer pop festival season, on the King's Dock. The work was similar to what I'd done in New York, really, and that experience was really important.

When we opened, I found myself running the basement restaurant, The Lower Place, underneath the hall doing the pre-concert and post-concert dining. Then we'd be doing the corporate hospitality for the big banks and lawyers and financial institutions.

We had all sorts of people pass through. One minute we'd have Jose Carreras and the next it would be the Buena Vista Social Club. After that, it would be Joan Baez and then it would be Elton John. The list was just crazy - and so exiting to do.

We'd have every genre of music, then a comedian, then The Human League. But it was good fun and my reputation in Liverpool started to evolve.

I cooked for the Queen at the Town Hall and sometime later for Condoleezza Rice, the USA Secretary of State.

The Philharmonic was the gateway to all sorts of things and we built a very happy team. I was very content there from 1995 until 2002, and then I moved to join The London Carriage Works and Hope Street Hotel team.

In the business plan, we wanted to become Liverpool's first boutique hotel and Liverpool's number 1 restaurant. That was the most exciting thing because it was what I'd dreamed of from when I first read New Classic Cuisine and got all those images in my mind of food to be proud of.

The London Carriage Works felt like the first time I could put my ideas on a plate and do what I thought was right. It was just before the Capital of Culture was announced so there was a huge level of excitement.

I had 12 great years there cooking for the stars and building a great reputation. I still love it to this day.

When I look back at the years at The London Carriage Works, I learned a huge amount.

It worked out well and I learned so much from that process, which equipped me for The Art School.

A business is almost a person in itself and that person needs looking after, even above yourself.

With The Art School, the concept was simple.

It was all about using those business lessons from The London Carriage Works and then doing the best food possible for the North West.

It was about showing that Liverpool has its own gastronomic culture. And it was about creating a place where people are prepared to pay for good food and where they can really enjoy it.

It was a joy to find the space because I know this area so well. I've been from the Philharmonic to The London Carriage Works and I know how things work.

From a design point of view, we got it right. We made the best use of the space in the Georgian Quarter.

I loved commissioning the artwork, Monsieur Mural, Matt Williams, and going to the auctions to get antiques that fit in every corner. And in a way, it's a bit like that with the food. I search and search.

We have a beef dish on. It's Galloway beef, from Heswall, on the Wirral, which is 13 miles away. It comes from an old Liverpool dish, beef and oyster pie. They used to go and collect the oysters because they couldn't afford the beef.

Basically, they would supplement the beef pie with the oysters because they didn't have enough protein to feed the family.

Then they learned that beef and oysters work really, really well together. And hence the pie came about.

Now the oysters are as expensive as the beef, or more so.

So for me, it's fascinating to have those sort of dishes. It's a dish featuring the cheek, the tongue and the sirloin and it's delicious. It's just one prime cut and the Cinderella cuts.

But those Cinderella cuts are the delicacies now and we show them off in a different way. For me, that's typical of our food because we're inspired by the seasons and the location.

We're inspired by my understanding of putting flavours together and that palette of textures and food.

Liverpool is the first city in the North of England to secure a prestigious partnership with the Royal Academy of Culinary Arts to train the Michelin-starred chefs of the future.

The City of Liverpool College has been hand-picked to work with restaurants across the North West to deliver Royal Academy of Culinary Arts (RACA) Chefs Apprenticeships, which are regarded as the gold standard for chef training in Europe.

I am among those who have helped to secure the coveted partnership and I am playing a key role in in its delivery through The Art School.

The course represents a unique opportunity for young chefs aged 16 to 19 to receive the highest level of training while working alongside top professionals at the finest restaurants and hotels. One day they might get to brush shoulders with celebrities from stage and screen - or turf.

I remember back to The London Carriage Works days, when we had a lot of the footballers stay with us. Rafa Benitez was managing Liverpool and he signed Xabi Alonso, so there was a strong connection with Spain and the Basque country.

On one occasion, they asked me to host a special dinner for Xabi and his friends, for his birthday.

The dinner was partly me and partly his favourite chef, Martin Berasategui, who is a three-star chef and whose restaurants hold eight stars in total. He was asked to cook at the Spanish Royal Wedding with Arzac, another three-star chef from San Sebastian.

So Martin was flown out to Liverpool and we did a joint tasting menu; he did four dishes and I did five dishes. It was recorded for the TV programme, Grub's Up, with Simon Rimmer.

Having a three-star chef in the kitchen was off the scale, it was hilarious as well as quite daunting. But Martin loved what we did and we learned so much from him.

I was lucky enough to meet him another time, on a different trip, and I asked him what inspired his dishes. He was laughing when he answered.

He said: 'This morning, I was walking my dog and it was February and over his shoulder I saw a hare'. And I looked over Martin's shoulder and there was another chef prepping a hare.

He said: 'It was Mother Nature's way of telling me it's time to have hare on the menu'. And I'll never forget that. It sounds dead, dead simple, but so many chefs forget that.

We have to listen to Mother Nature. On that occasion, it was hare. For us, it might be fish or veg or meat. And you only get to tune into Mother Nature by working and cooking and handling produce every day.

I bring dishes back now that I may have written 10 years ago. But they come back in a different form.

I know when to put red mullet on the menu, or saffron. It's absolutely about the ingredients and listening to Mother Nature. We couldn't have asparagus last week, for instance, we had to wait an extra week because it had been too cold.

But we had skate on the menu because a local boat went off into the Dee Estuary and just so happened to get a load of skate. It sounds simple but so few chefs do that.

My travels influence my food, of course. There might be a bit of Singapore in a turbot dish, which features mango; or lamb with a little bit of tabbouleh, which is redolent of Dubai.

There might be a bit of America here, or Poland there. That's how I've developed and how all chefs develop.

It's the experience and travel, it's watching other chefs and tasting produce when it's at its best. In the final analysis, our job is quite simple.

It's to seek out the finest ingredients, to create an hospitable atmosphere and to present the food at its absolute best.

That's what we're devoted to here at The Art School. And we hope that you enjoy it.

Paul Askew

October 2017

How to make a dish

I've found five simple words to encapsulate my philosophy of food. Here they are: "What grows together goes together." Land and sea combinations really work well too, as do foods from specific regions and seasons.

If you're looking for a great accompaniment to game, for instance, what's better than the sweet flavours of autumnal fruit, with balance and acidity of course?

If you want a beautiful wine to accompany spicy Spanish flavours, what better than a vintage that shared the same, hot, vertile soil. If you want to pair delicious cutlets of Saltmarsh lamb, what better than the sea wild herbs that grow round and about?

The seasons tell us what we should cook. They are our guide. We look to cook the best of local produce when it's in peak condition.

So when we're in the weeks before spring starts to blossom, we're looking ahead and thinking of how to cook asparagus and artichokes, beans and beets, rhubarb and ramps, strawberries and sweet onions.

And so it goes through the year as we follow nature's larder, making the most of spring, summer, autumn and winter.

I visualise a dish first, thinking about how it will look on the plate. Presentation is important. Diners engage all of their senses and so attractive food always seems to taste better.

Flavour, however, is the key component. And we're looking for dishes that marry well, that feature ingredients that are complimentary and dovetail well.

Seasonings should be spot on, to enhance natural flavours. And we'll also be thinking about what wines work well with particular dishes. The greatest dishes will have a good, even balance between protein, carbohydrates and vegetables.

We don't want to overload diners with carbs, though a little starch adds to a dish. And the sauce is all important.

We work hard to provide an accompaniment that dazzles and delights, that adds a flavoursome flourish.

Integrity is everything. We love the Cinderella cuts of meat, for instance; the ones that take a little longer to cook, that require a slow braise and that melt in the mouth. And we believe that we should respect the produce in our kitchen: it's been grown, reared, caught and harvested with love by an exceptional, artisan producer and it's our duty to treat it well.

I sketch out dishes before cooking. Then I'll test and test and test, adjusting the balance and tweaking the seasonings, playing with the presentation until it's spot on.

When we get it right, when the flavours are harmonious and when the food is as pretty as a picture, it's heaven on a plate.

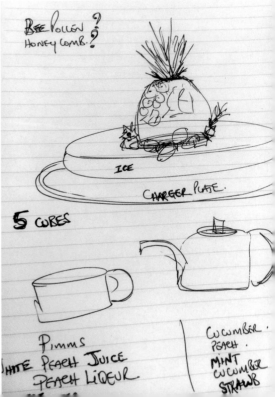

33

THE LITTLE
WONDER
WINS
5TH TITLE

Producers

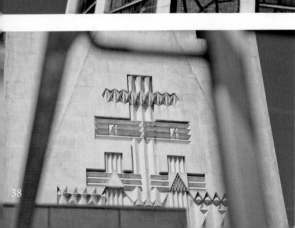

Two Cathedrals Honey

A pioneering conservation project led to the creation of one of Liverpool's most beautiful and unique products.

Two Cathedrals Honey came about when the city's two cathedrals joined forces to help halt the decline in the UK bee population.

Hives were placed in the grounds of the two cathedrals, producing an excellent crop of local honey.

Rich in flavour and perfectly pure, it's an ingredient that we're proud to use at The Art School.

As a city, we can take great pride in the cathedrals for engaging in the project – the only two in the UK that do.

The honey is the work of beekeeper John Moran, who was fireman during the Toxteth riots in 1981 and later became a teacher. He was inspired by the work of former bishops, Anglican David Sheppard and Roman Catholic Derek Warlock, who promoted unity in Liverpool.

As John walked along Hope Street one day, he remembered the work that the bishops had done to promote community cohesion – and the idea for Two Cathedrals Honey came to him.

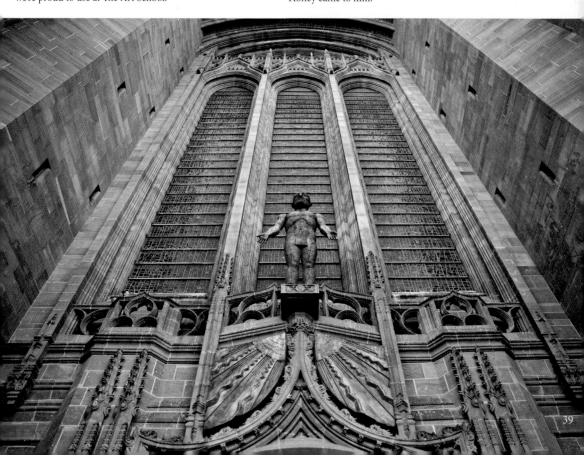

Wirral Watercress – Peter Jones

Housed in the greenhouses of a former bedding plant suppliers, Peter Jones started Wirral Water Cress from scratch just over 11 years ago.

Peter left the family farm to set up on his own selling watercress and other salads to restaurants and the wholesale trade.

The day starts when the sun comes up and lasts long into the evening. Peter says: "I think most people work 9 to 5, I work 5-9, with 5am the start and 9pm the finish."

Peter's main crop is watercress and rocket, which dominates a large proportion of his greenhouses. In addition he also cultivates wild garlic, sorrel, wild strawberries and a range of other salads, edible flowers and vegetables. It's an amazing asset to have a man like Peter onside to basically grow to order.

Several hives are dotted in-between the greenhouses for Peter's honeybees. Production stops in December, January, February where the greenhouses are washed down and everything is prepared and re-set for the growing season ahead.

44

Wards Fishmongers

Simon and Nigel Buckmaster are fourth generation fishmongers. They were always destined to follow into the family business after Wards was first established in 1927 by Emily Ward, the wife of a ship's cook from Birkenhead.

Wards was first located in Borough Road until the late 60s, moving to the old market in 1974. It transferred to its current location in Birkenhead market in the mid 1970s.

There's a real passion for seafood, evidenced by a daily 4am start, with the last orders often coming in at 1am in the morning. Simon and Nigel follow the different seasons for fish, sharing the view that you should only have the fish when it's at its very best. That can mean fish like plaice are off the menu for three months.

The business supplies over three tonnes of fish and shellfish a week to restaurants and the public across the North West.

There are daily calls with Simon to discuss the best fish in the market and availability for the week ahead. The quality and integrity of the produce is fantastic and we love working with the guys at Wards Fishmongers.

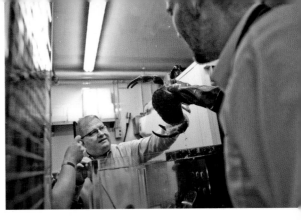
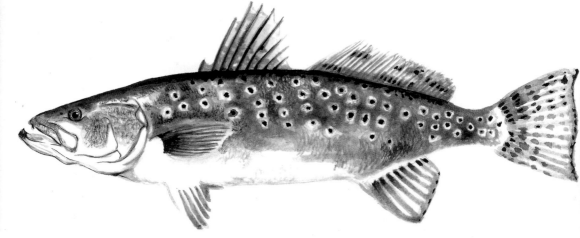

Senna Lane Farm

Senna Lane Farm was built by the current owners' family in 1859 and extended in the early 1900s. Nestled in the picturesque West Cheshire village of Comberbach the farm is home to Hebridean and Herdwick flocks, a small beef herd and a delightful quartet of saddleback pigs. Chickens and ducks wander the farmyard stables, outbuildings and courtyard in these delightful surroundings.

Liz Thomas grew up on the farm with her parents, who moved there in 1958 after they were married. Liz returned to the farm, having earned a degree in agriculture at Bangor University and briefly lectured there. She also lectured at colleges in Shropshire and Nantwich.

Farming is very much in the blood and Liz returned to the farm with her husband, a sheep farmer from Mid-Wales, to start her own family. The farm was an organic dairy farm for many many years, but following the tragedy of foot and mouth the decision was taken to sell the herd and downsize.

A small beef herd that Liz looks after for other farmers, still graces Senna Lane but it's the Herdwick and Hebridean flocks that provide the majority of the daily management. Ably supported by her daughter, Emma, a postgraduate studying at The University of Liverpool, Liz's animals are kept in outstanding condition.

The slow growing Hebridean are popular with the local Wildlife Trust who use them to manage grazing across areas of outstanding natural beauty throughout the county.

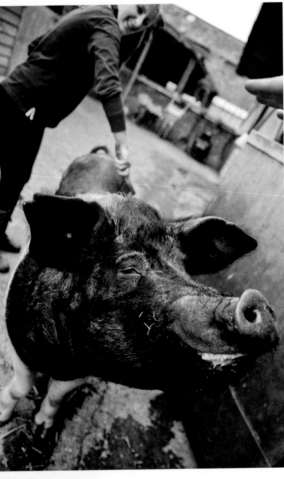

The Rhug Estate

Lord Newborough, the owner of The Rhug Estate, in Corwen, Denbighshire, is a great example of what can be achieved by those who work with a sense of purpose.

Lord Newborough strives towards a more sustainable future. His vision has seen the conversion of his farm to organic, the addition of a large portfolio of renewable energy projects, and continued support for local Welsh produce.

Rhug Estate covers 12,500 acres extending from Gwyddelwern in the north, Carrog to the east, Cynwyd to the south and Maerdy to the west.

The 6,700 acre in-hand organic farm is the geographical core of the estate along with Rûg Mansion being the main residence.

The Glynllifon Estate comprises of 7500 acres which includes the main in-hand faming enterprise of Ty Mawr.

The remainder of the estate has about 170 tenancies including: let farms, in hand and let forestry, let cottages, commercial premises and storage, traditional sporting including shooting and fishing, modern sports such as rally car driving, gorge walking, mountain biking, canoeing and public events.

The quality of the estate and the energy poured into maintenance reflects in the sumptuous produce that it produces.

The Rhug Estate has won many accolades, including a raft of golds from the Guild of Fine Food Great Taste Awards.

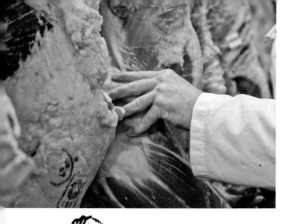

Claremont Farm

The Pimbleys are a family of farmers, growing and selling their own fruit and vegetables on the Wirral since 1906.

They champion local produce by putting their favourites in the farm shop and they celebrate their work during much-loved food and drink festivals. Their work helps to reconnect children with their food, how it's grown and what it tastes like.

A farm shop also connects them with the wider public, offering a butchers' counter and café in the heart of the Wirral countryside.

The farm has been ahead of the game for generations: Grandfather Pimbley was the first to diversify, introducing a farm shop more than 40 years ago following his return from a trip to the USA where he witnessed pick-your-own for the first time.

Ian Pimbley carried on the tradition by developing the range of vegetables grown, including award-winning asparagus from 1994 (adored by Chef Askew).

Andrew and his brother Guy have followed in those footsteps, taking the farm into an Environmental Stewardship Scheme that welcomes more than 3,000 kids each year.

Both men have children of their own and hope to pass down the reigns of Claremont to another generation of Pimbleys.

Edge & Son

My 'perfect 10' score on BBC's Great British Menu came with Callum Edge's Hebridean hogget. I named the dish 'Summer memories with Marjorie', after my mother. To me, it was a way of honouring and loving her through my cooking – an edible tribute to her and the things she loved to eat in the summer.

When you bring together such important emotional and professional things like that to be judged by some of the best chefs in Britain and on national television, then each element has to be absolutely right.

When it comes to meat, that means everything about the animal: its breed; its diet and environment and its life and death.

Edge & Son have been trading on the banks of the Mersey, father to son (& daughters in law), for over 170 years. Same family, same shop – an unbroken line of unparalleled knowledge and craft.

Callum supplies many of the best restaurants in the North West (my own included) for fine dining. Ok, so we're not talking about the most inexpensive food. But I ask people to remember that what makes us compatible businesses is our mutual belief in the best possible, free-range, extensively farmed, rare and native breed animals. Those cost a little more to produce. .

We also believe in training the next generations of butchers and chefs in how to make the best of every part of the animal – from nose to tail – and in that way honouring it. Every chef who works for me is put through Edge's butchery masterclass, which deepens their respect for the meat and really enhances their skills.

Callum says: "For me, it's not about what is the best cut, but what is the best animal, and we use all of it with the same respect and passion."

Marjorie would have loved him for that.

Recipes

Spring

Warm Salad of Honey-glazed Roasted Fig, Spring Leaves & Tymsboro Goat's Cheese

Serves: 4

Ingredients:

Figs and Goat's Cheese

4 figs - 1 per plate cut into quarters
3 croutes of focaccia bread per portion
Walnuts - 5 halves per plate, roasted and crushed
Maldon salt
Caster sugar
Two Cathedrals Honey
Blood orange puree (please see glossary)
Tymsboro goat's cheese

Method:

- Using your focaccia, cut your bread into 4cm cubes and brush them with a pastry brush using melted unsalted butter and a drizzling of extra virgin olive oil. Bake them in the oven on 180 degrees for about five minutes until they turn golden brown
- Coat your walnuts using sugar and salt and roast them in the oven until they are golden. Remove them from the oven and allow them to cool before roughly chopping them for a garnish
- Quarter your figs and lay them on a flat tray and drizzle them with your honey and a little sugar, and place them under the grill to dissolve the sugar and allow the natural sugars to caramelise. Ensure the fruit is perfectly ripe with no blemishes. It is imperative that the fruit isn't over ripe and becoming soft otherwise it will break down during the cooking process
- Slice the cheese at this stage to go on top of your focaccia and place under the grill to melt

Salad

Nasturtium
Watercress
Frisée
Red chicory

Method:

- The most important thing is to use seasonal leaves that give different flavours, textures and preferably colours. This will give the salad an extra depth and make it look more attractive
- The vinaigrette will bring all the components together by adding acidity

Vinaigrette

50ml extra virgin olive oil
20ml good quality white wine vinegar
Tsp Dijon mustard
Pinch of Maldon sea salt
Pinch of sugar

Method:

- Add all of your ingredients to a bowl except the oil and mix them together
- Slowly add the oil, continuously whisking it until it combines and creates an emulsion

Assembly

Drizzle some of your lovely honey around the plate and scatter your crushed nuts in the centre. Assemble your goats cheese toast, and add your fig on top. In-between the toast add your shards of chicory, and then gradually add your remaining leaves ensuring that your create some height. Finish by dotting your puree. Nasturtium leaf, and marigold flowers are often used to decorate this dish

Chef's Recommended Wine:

Podere Castorani, Cadetto, Cerasuolo D' Abruzzo, Italy, 2016

Fillet of Menai Mackerel, Blood Orange Dressing & Herb Infused Goats Curd

Serves: 4

Ingredients:

Mackerel

2 Fillets of Menai mackerel (Anglesey) cut into half and pin-boned
2-3 medium golden beetroot, peeled and 2.5 cm cubed dice 3 cubes per plate. These are blanched in saffron and vegetable stock to enhance the colour and flavour
Fish seasoning (please see glossary)
1 sheet of silicone paper for grilling
Splash of vegetable oil

Method:

- It is very important that we retain the lovely shine and colour of this fish. Therefore we grill it on some oiled silicone paper skin-side down
- The skin is seasoned with a little salt, however, the flesh side will be seasoned using the fish seasoning in the glossary section
- Place under grill for 2 minutes before removing from heat

Goats Curd

Curthwaite goat's curd
Lemon zest and juice
Bunch of chives

Method:

- Into a bowl, combine all of the ingredients, and mix them together until it is smooth
- This will ensure consistency for when it is piped
- Adjust the seasoning and put into a piping bag with a nozzle ready for plating

Hooton Watercress Puree

150 g Hooton watercress
2.3g Maldon salt
0.23g Xantham gum
Iced water
Fresh ground black pepper to taste

Method:

- Blanch watercress in boiling salted water for 30 seconds
- Place straight into iced water. Drain and dry when cool
- Add to a Thermomix and puree with pepper, salt and xantham gum
- Place in a squeezy bottle and chill to serve

Blood Orange Dressing

1 blood orange - half squeezed for juice and half filleted for garnish
1 banana shallot peeled and finely diced
1 tsp whole grain mustard
Splash of white wine vinegar
Pinch of sugar
Maldon salt
Pepper
20ml extra virgin olive oil

Method:

- Add all of your ingredients to a bowl except the oil and the orange, and then mix them together
- Slowly add the oil, continuously whisking it until it combines and creates an emulsion
- Add the juice of the orange and the small orange fillets at the end

Salad

Picked Hooton watercress
Frisée
Radish
Sweet red onion - thinly sliced
Sunflower shoots

Method:

- The most important thing to us is that you use seasonal leaves that give different flavours, textures and preferably colours
- This will give the salad an extra depth, both visually and to taste. In this case we have used watercress for a pepper taste, Frisée for bitterness
- Use sweet red onions for savoury notes, sunflower shoots for some sweetness and radish for crunch. This will balance out the flavours and the textures of the dish. Vinaigrette will bring all the components together by adding acidity

Blood Orange Puree

Please see glossary page

Assembly

Plate as seen here in the picture

Chef's Recommended Wine:

Fromm La Strada, Sauvignon Blanc, Marlborough New Zealand, 2015

North Sea Haddock with Brown Shrimp & Herb Crust, Pickled Cucumber & Mustard

Serves: 4

Ingredients:

Fish

4 haddock fillets - 120g loin end per portion

Method:

- Prepare and portion the haddock fillet

Fish Stock

Fish stock (see glossary)
70ml double cream
1 tbsp whole grain mustard
50g butter

Method:

- Reduce the fish stock down (See the fish stock recipe) and add the cream and mustard
- Finish with the butter and pour this into a squirty bottle ready to serve

Crust

50g brown shrimps
100g breadcrumbs
20g parmesan
50g parsley
20g dill
3g freshly ground mace
3g freshly ground nutmeg
1 lemon - zested
Pinch of white pepper
Pinch of salt

Method:

- In a blender, add the breadcrumbs, parsley, dill, salt, pepper, mace, nutmeg, parmesan and potted shrimp, including the zest of the lemon.
- Blend it all together until it is fine before adding the melted butter. Roll this mixture out to 2mm thick between 2 sheets of greaseproof and leave in on a tray in the fridge to set
- Once the herb crust is set, portion it by cutting it into the right shape to sit on top of the fish. Place the fish on to a tray ready to bake. Place in the oven on 160 degrees for three or four minutes, depending on the size of your fillet

Leeks

150g leeks
1 cucumber
50ml white balsamic vinegar
300ml fish stock
50ml cream
10g whole grain mustard

Method:

- Prepare the leeks by cutting them into julienne and place them in a tub ready to serve
- Cook the leeks in a pan with the cut-offs of haddock, and add the butter and fish sauce, and finish it be seasoning
- Using a solferino baller, cut out the balls from the cucumber and place them into the balsamic vinegar
- Season them and place them into a tub ready for service

Assembly

On a bed of the leeks and flaked haddock place the baked shrimp, crusted haddock. Arrange the pickled cucumbers and top with sturgeon caviar or Keta.

Chef's Recommended Wine:

Lagar De Bouza, Albarino, Rias Baixas, Spain, 2016

Breast of Goosnargh Duckling with Rhubarb, Beetroot & Burnt Orange Purees

Serves: 4

Ingredients:

Duck

4 breasts (180g each) of Goosnargh duck, trimmed and scored
Duck seasoning (please see glossary)

Method:

● Season the skin of the duck using the duck seasoning. Using a cold pan, add the breasts to the pan skin-side down. No fat is needed in this pan due to the natural fats of the duck
● As the fat renders down, turn the breast over. This usually takes about 2- 3 minutes
● Cook this for another 2- 3 minutes, and leave it to rest on a wire rack to retain all of the natural juices
● Ensure that you don't overcook the duck and serve it a beautiful medium-rare

Potatoes

4 medium potatoes - peeled, cubed in 2.5 cm
400ml duck fat
2 sprigs of thyme
1 bay leaf
5 peppercorns

Method:

● In a pan or a skillet, colour each side of the potato before placing them into the duck fat with the herbs, and cooking them on a low heat until tender
● Drain the potatoes, and place them onto a baking tray. Finish them in the oven on 150 degrees for 10-15 minutes (depending on the variety of potato), until they are crisp
● Here at The Art School, the variety of potato that we use for this dish is "Victoria" potatoes, which are sourced locally from Claremont Farm

Garnish

4 navet, or mini turnip, peeled and blanched, halved
4 spring onions, peeled and washed
1 baby gem lettuce, cut into ¼ lengthways
80g peas, blanched
80g Feves (broad beans), blanched with the pods removed

Method:

● Into a hot pan, add the baby gem lettuce and spring onion with some seasoning. This will give the ingredients a lovely charring effect and texture
● Add the beans and peas to a bowl ready to reheat in a little melted butter and vegetable stock

Honey

Two Cathedrals honey, infused with lavender from chef's garden

Natural Jus

Please see glossary
Macerate with Fresh Blackberries

Rhubarb Puree

Please see glossary

Burnt Orange Puree

Please see glossary

Assembly

For the plating of this dish, centre the charred baby gem lettuce, with the sliced breast on top slightly to the side. That is brushed with the lovely lavender-infused honey. Decorate your plate using your cubes of crispy potato, and dots of both your purees. The dish is completed with the peas, beans and navet, with the macerated blackberries tying it together.

Chef's Recommended Wine:

Odfjell, Armador Carmenere, Maipo Valley, Chile 2013

Confit Leg & Breast of Organic Rhug Estate Chicken & Claremont Farm Asparagus

Serves: 4

Ingredients:

Confit leg and breast Rhug Estate chicken

Breast and leg of organic Rhug Estate chicken (1/2 breast and a leg parcel per person)
Chicken seasoning (Please see the glossary)
Chicken stock (please see the glossary)

Method:

- At the restaurant we buy whole chickens as it fits with the philosophy of our cuisine to use everything that we possibly can from such a precious ingredient as organic chicken
- The drumstick and thighs are used for confit before being pulled and shredded for the parcel garnish
- The skin is used for making the chicken crackling, and the breast is pan-roasted as the prime cut
- Dust the chicken using the seasoning, both on the skin and within the butterfly
- If you are cooking this at home, it is more beneficial to cook the whole crown of chicken in the oven with the meat still attached. This is because the cage of the bird will retain lots of natural juices into the meat
- At the restaurant we remove the breast from the bone as we don't know how many portions we might cook to order during service and we don't want to be wasteful
- Place the cut into a lightly-oiled pan meat-side down to seal, before turning the breast over to reveal the skin and place into the oven for 4-5 minutes on 165 degrees until it is just cooked. This will keep the breast juicy and moist. Rest for 5 minutes until ready to carve

Sauce

Claremont Farm asparagus, 3 spears per portion peeled and trimmed then cooked in boiling salted water at the last minute
Morelles, 3 per portion. Brushed and trimmed ready to sauté in a splash of vegetable oil and butter
3 or 4 shavings of summer truffles per plate, shaved on top of the chicken during the plating
Chopped tarragon and truffle trimmings for the natural jus.
(We use the double strength chicken stock, see details opposite for stock for confit leg parcel, which is infused with truffles and tarragon.)

Method:

- See method of stock for confit leg parcel

Cyprus (Spunta) Potato

2 large Spunta potatoes, washed and peeled, cut into dice
Extra virgin olive oil
Maldon sea salt

Method:

- Cook the potatoes until soft in salted boiling water
- Drain them, before drying off any excess water by returning them to the pan and placing them back on the heat for a minute or two. Pass through drum sieve to ensure a smooth puree
- Add a drizzle of olive oil and season well for taste

Confit Leg Parcel

Fuille de Bric pastry- 2 sheets cut in half to make four parcels
Chopped parsley
1 tbsp natural Jus
Shredded leg meat
1 egg yolk
10g unsalted butter
A splash of vegetable oil
Poppy seeds

Stock for Confit Leg Parcel

500ml chicken stock, please see the glossary
Mirepoix of vegetables, 1 carrot, 1 leek, 1 onion, 1 celery stick
2 cloves of peeled garlic
175ml good quality white wine
Bouquet garni
5 black peppercorns
Tsp fennel seeds
Maldon sea salt
Ground white pepper

Method:

- Seal the leg and thigh in a hot pan ensuring the browning and colouration of the meat
- Place into a deep roasting tin, along with the chicken stock, the mirepoix of vegetables, the wine, garlic, bouquet garni, peppercorns, fennel seeds and seasoning
- Slow cook this for two hours on 150 degrees until the meat is so tender it looks like that it is just about to fall apart
- Pass off the liquor, which will now be of double strength, through a muslin cloth into a pan and reduce it down with a knob of butter to give it a nice sheen. Finish this jus using the trimmings of truffle and chopped tarragon leaves

Assembly

Plate all elements before adding the jus.

Chef's Recommended Wine:

Waterkloof, Circumstance Chenin Blanc, Stellenbosch, South Africa 2014

A Plate of Callum's Oldfield Farm Galloway Beef to include Tongue, Cheek & Sirloin

Serves: 4

Ingredients:

Plate of beef

50g cooked shredded cheek
25g tongue sliced (ideally pre-brined by the butcher)
100g sirloin per portion

Method:

- For the sirloin we prefer to buy it on the bone and we use everything including the fat which is rendered down so that it can be used during the cooking process for the cooking of the beef, the tongue, the cheek and the vegetables.
- The bones are then used to make the beef stock. Please see the making of the stock on the glossary page
- If you don't feel comfortable with preparation of the sirloin, you could ask your local butcher for two 200g medallions. These will be cooked and cut in half, thus creating 4 portions suitable to plate as per our photograph.

Tongue

Ingredients:

Cooked ox tongue, from your butcher, or whole tongue
If using whole tongue, you'll need a mirepoix of vegetables and bouquet garni in which to cook it

Method:

- The easiest way to achieve results in the home kitchen is to ask for cooked ox tongue from your butcher, but make sure they don't slice it. Then you can cut it into appropriate-sized pieces at home
- If you want to cook it at home, you'll simmer it as you would a ham
- Cook it through in a mirepoirx of vegetables with bouquet garni and herbs, until tender. The cooking time will depend on the size of the tongue. Simmer slowly. A whole tongue will take two to three hours. Use such herbs as thyme, parsley stalks and bay leaf. When the tongue is cooked, reduce the stock for your jus

Cheek

Ingredients:

500ml Beef Stock, please see the glossary
Mirepoix of vegetables, 1 Carrot, 1 Leek, 1 Onion, 1 Celery Stick
2 Cloves of Peeled Garlic
175ml Deep Red Wine
Bouquet Gani

5 Black Peppercorns
Tsp Fennel Seeds
Maldon Sea Salt
Ground White Pepper

Method:

- Remove all of the fat and excess sinew from the cheek, and seal them in a hot pan with a knob of butter. Place the cheeks into a deep roasting tin along with the beef stock, the mirepoix of vegetables, the wine, garlic, bouquet garni, peppercorns, fennel seeds and seasoning.
- Slow cook for four hours on 150 degrees until the meat is so tender it looks like it is just about to fall apart. Pass off the liquor through a muslin cloth into a pan and reduce it with the natural juices of the oysters and a knob of butter to give it a nice sheen.
- Add the shredded cheek to a pan and coat it with a little of the sauce to bind it together before presenting it in the clean oyster shell with a spoon of sauce over the top.

Beans

100g Turtle Beans
Brunoise of vegetables including carrot, leek, celery and banana shallot
25g Unsalted Butter

Method:

- Place the pre-cooked turtle beans in boiling salted water for 15 minutes. Refresh ready to serve.
- Sweat the vegetables in the butter before adding the beans.
- Finish with 50ml natural jus (see page in the glossary)

Oysters

4 Rock Oysters (Menai or Colchester)

Method:

- Steam with the juices retained, and the bottom shell retained for presentation. (They should be steamed for approximately 2-3 minutes so that they don't overcook. This is to ensure that they don't gain a rubbery texture and an unpleasant taste).

- Continues over

Spring - Mains

- Continued from previous

Cauliflower Cous Cous

1/3 Cauliflower, Grated/ Food Processed
½ Lemon, Squeezed
20g Chopped Chives
Seasoning

Method:

- In the food processor, add the cauliflower and blitz to a chunky breadcrumb consistency. Add a squeeze of fresh lemon juice, the chopped chives, and season to taste. Mix together and place in the fridge until ready to use.
- Using the remainder of the cauliflower, blanche the remaining florettes in a pan of boiling salted water to two minutes. Then remove placing directly into iced water to stop the cooking process.
- Drain the florettes on some kitchen cloth to rid of any excess water. Cut lengthways down each florettete to create a flat surface. When all elements are ready to be plated, add the florettes to a hot cast iron pan with a splash of oil to char the surface. Finish with a knob of butter and use to garnish the final dish.

Vegetable Garnish

1 large Carrot
1 large Courgette

Method:

- Slice vegetables on a mandolin into ribbons.
- Toss in a little herb butter.

Assembly

This is all about Liverpool's tradition of beef and oyster. Place three elements on the dish, the tongue on two spoonfuls of the turtle beans go together. The oyster shell is filled with beef cheek topped with a poached oyster sat on the cauliflower cous cous. Finally the ribbon vegetables with that perfect piece of rested sirloin and to finish drizzle with the jus from the cheek.

Chef's Recommended Wine:

Spioenkop 1900 Pinotage, Elgin, South Africa 2015

Valhrona Dark Chocolate Bordelou, Mango Foam, Matcha Green Tea Sorbet & Cremeux

Serves: 4

Ingredients:

Honey Cremeux

3g gelatine, softened
3 egg yolks
35g caster sugar
225g double Cream
58g honey

Method:

- Place the honey and cream in two separate pans and bring to the boil. Meanwhile, in a bowl, whisk the eggs and sugar together until light and fluffy. Bloom the gelatine in cold water
- Once the cream and honey are boiling, add the cream to the honey slowly. Add the gelatine at this point and then pour 1/3 of the mix into the eggs. Pour egg mix back into the pan
- Bring the mix to 75 degrees, constantly mixing with a spatula to avoid the mix catching the bottom of the pan and scrambling.
- Pass the mix through a chinoix and leave to cool. Set in the fridge. Once cold, beat with a wooden spoon to get a smooth cremeux and place in a piping bag ready for service.

Dark Chocolate Cremeux

250g cream
250g milk
100g egg yolk
50g sugar
240g 70% dark chocolate - Guanaja Valhrona

Method:

- Heat up the milk in a pan to boiling point. While this is boiling, whisk the eggs and sugar together before then pouring a 1/3rd of the milk into the egg mix
- Then pour that back into the pan, and place it back on the heat and bring to 83 degrees while stirring constantly
- Pour the mix over the chocolate through a sieve to melt the chocolate
- Once melted, mix it together and place it into an airtight tub to set in the fridge

Hazlenut Bordelou Cake

450g hazlenuts
300g caster sugar
300g butter
20g cocoa powder
50g melted dark chocolate
60g semolina
6 eggs

Method:

- Using the paddle on Kitchen Aid, cream together butter and sugar until light and fluffy. Then slowly add in the egg
- Sift the cocoa powder and ground almonds together and then fold it into the sugar and egg mix
- Pour the mixture into the baking tray and bake it in the oven for 13 minutes on 160 degrees until cooked
- Remove from the oven and leave it to cool on a wire rack
- Portion the cake as per the photograph, into 2 cm squares

Mango Foam

150g mango puree
0.7g Versa whip
0.7g Xanthan Gum

Method:

- Place the mango puree, xanthan gum and versa whip into the Kitchen Aid bowl with the whisk attachment and whisk on a highspeed until it is light and fluffy.

Green Tea Sorbet

30g green tea
550ml water
150g sugar
60g glucose
75g Pro sorbet

Method:

- Heat up all of the ingredients in a pan, and bring them to the boil. Bring the pan off the heat, and place a lid on pan so that you can leave the contents to infuse for an hour. Pass this through a chinois and then freeze it in a Paco beaker for 24 hours at -22° degrees.

Matcha Powder

- Using a sieve, dust the powder on top on the dessert when plated up

Assembly

To serve this dessert, arrange three pieces of sponge on the plate, and quenelle the green tea sorbet and place this on top of the centre sponge. Decorate the final plate with dots of the chocolate cremeux and the mango foam, and a dusting of matcha powder to finish.

Chef's Recommended Wine:

Fernando de Castilla, Pedro Ximinez Antique, Jerez, Spain

The Captain's Trophy

Serves: 4

Ingredients:

Pineapple

3-4 baby pineapple (top & tail peeled and cubed for roasting)
1 punnet of strawberries in quarters
1 punnet wild strawberries
1 x 227g jar Two Cathedrals Honey
75g Two Cathedrals bee pollen
200g light muscovado sugar
70ml Dark Matter Rum
250g premium unsalted butter
12 free range eggs
250g caster sugar
Borage flower
Begonia (Apple blossom flower)
Mexican Marigold
Pineapple mint – The Art School

Method:

● Prepare 3-4 baby pineapples, topped, tailed and carefully diced ready for roasting
● In a bowl mix the pineapple cubes with the Muscovado sugar, dark matter rum and some fresh vanilla.
● Place on a non-stick tray and roast in a 170° oven for about 8-10minutes until just starting to golden brown
● Allow to cool. Select the most perfect cubes for the dressing of the dish, 3 per plate, using the rest of the pineapple and juices to make a puree which in turn is used in the clotted cream ice cream as the ripple
● Retain some of the juices to brush the honey sponge

Ice Cream (Clotted cream recipe - measurement 1-1.3 litre)

565ml whole milk
160ml double cream
125g sugar
60g egg yolk
40g dextrose
50g skimmed milk powder
75-100ml of Rhodda's clotted cream

Method:

● Warm the milk and cream in a pan
● Whisk the sugar and egg yolks into a smooth ribbon stage before pouring into the warmed milk (not boiling)
● Whisk and return to the heat to make a traditional Sauce Anglais mix.
● Add the remainder of the ingredients to the mix continually stirring the mix gently
● Churn the ice cream in an ice cream maker for approximately 1 hour 30 minutes until smooth and setting.

Honey Sponge (For the base)

250g unsalted butter
250g caster sugar
200g self-raising flour
50g ground almonds
6 eggs
50g warm Two Cathedrals Honey to brush onto sponge
1/2tsp ground ginger

Method:

● Cream the butter and caster sugar together in a bowl until blended together
● Add the eggs and mix until smooth (using a Kitchen Aid)
● Gently fold the flour, ground almonds and ground ginger to make the sponge mix
● Pour the cake mixture into a buttered silicone paper lined baking tray approximately 6-7cm deep
● Bake in a pre-heated oven at 160 degrees for 15-20 minutes until lightly golden and moist
● Brush with the honey whilst warm and portion accordingly for the Alaska

Italian Meringue

3 egg whites
240g caster sugar
2 drops of coconut essence (Heera)
2 drops Pinya Sosa (Pineapple Aroma)
½ demitasse spoon egg yellow powder (Heera)
100ml cold water

Method:

● Dissolve the caster sugar in the cold water by bringing to the boil to reach 118 degrees (checked by temperature probe)
● Whisk the egg whites in the Kitchen Aid to a point where the volume is increasing
● Slowly add the sugar syrup to cook out the egg white and increase the volume to a peak
● As this is happening add the coconut essence and pineapple aroma

Granola

250g oats (Toasted)
50g honey
50g nibbed almonds
Tspn bee pollen
25g linseeds
50g crushed hazlenuts

Method:

● Combine the ingredients

● Continues over

Spring - Desserts

- Continued from previous

Wimbledon Pimms Iced Tea

A refreshing accompaniment for the Captain's Trophy or a palate cleansing pre-dessert.

For 5 Demitasse cups

125 ml Classic Pimms
125ml Iced Tea (Milky Oolong)
50ml Peach Syrup (Giffard)
25ml Funkin white peach puree
25ml Lemon

Garnish

Cucumber
Mint leaf
Borage flower
Orange zest
Strawberry

- Shake over ice in a Boston shaker and double strain
- Serve from the chosen teapot – prohibition style.

Assembly

Scatter the granola in a circular fashion with the meringue sitting to the centre. Decorate with strawberries and mint.

Chef's Recommended Wine:

Ditch the wine and enjoy your summer fruit cup

Crème Brûlée

Serves: 12

Ingredients:

Crème brûlée

793g cream
252g whole milk
250g sugar
250g white chocolate
16 egg yolks
2 vanilla pods

Method:

- Place the milk, cream and all the spices into a large pan and bring to the boil
- While it heats up separate your eggs and put all the yolks into a bowl
- Weigh the chocolate in another bowl big enough to hold all of the cream mixture
- Add your sugar to the egg yolks and whisk together. Don't add the sugar to the bowl and leave it standing because that will cause the egg yolk to crystalize
- Once the cream and milk have come to the boil add it to the yolk mix. Now, using a spatula, mix together. Don't use a whisk
- Once combined put the brûlée mix back into the pan and bring the mix to 83 degrees. Using the spatula, keep mixing it. Don't let the mix stand still or it will overheat at the bottom of the pan and split
- Once it reaches 83 degrees, pass through a chinois into the white chocolate. Let it stand for about 3 minutes and then mix together with the spatula again
- Pour into the lined moulds and bake for about 15 minutes on 100 degrees with no fan. Check on them after that: they should need about 5 minutes extra. Look out for the sexy wobble

White Chocolate Crumb

200g white chocolate

- Bake for 5 minutes until light golden brown. Let it cool down and then blitz lightly. If you over-blend the oils will come out and it will be too wet to use

Brandy Snap

55g golden syrup
50g plain flour
55g butter
55g sugar

- Mix the golden syrup, butter and sugar into a pan and melt all together. Once all melted add the sifted flour and mix together
- Spread on a tray thinly and bake on 180 degrees for 5 minutes until golden brown

Assembly

Dress with seasonal fruit and micro herbs to finish.

Chef's Recommended Wine:

Château Coutet, Barsac, 1970

Summer

Cornish Red Mullet with Lemon, Parsley & Brown Shrimp Risotto and Pastis Sauce

Serves: 4

Ingredients:

Cornish red mullet

4 fillets of red mullet (100g per fillet), descaled and pin-boned (retain the head and the bones to make the fish stock)

Method:

● To prepare and cook the mullet, place four portions skin-side down onto an oiled baking parchment sheet, and place under the grill for approximately 1 ½ minutes
● Remove fish from under the grill and plate to serve

Potatoes (For the Rice-less Risotto)

2 large Spunta potatoes, peeled and washed, ½ cm cubed and blanched in the saffron stock
1 pot of Southport potted shrimps
1 healthy pinch of Cheshire saffron (pre-soaked in hot water)
Splash of sunflower oil
50g freshly grated parmesan
50g unsalted butter

Method:

● Add the potted shrimp to the potatoes, season, and add olive oil until it reaches the desired consistency and flavour
● Finish with chopped chives and grated of parmesan
● Use a splash of organic extra virgin olive oil to garnish around the risotto

Fish Seasoning

See Glossary

Pastis Mullet sauce

2kg of mullet bones & heads
5 plum tomatoes cut in half
1/2 lemon
Bouquet garni
Mirepoix of vegetables (2 carrots, 2 onions, 2 celery sticks, 1 fennel bulb, 3 garlic cloves)
150ml Pastis
250ml cream
5 white peppercorns, 10 fennel seeds, and 2 bay leaves
1 ltr of fish stock

Method:

● Roast the mullet bones for 30 minutes in the oven, and then turn them over after 20 minutes
● Sweat the mirepoix with olive oil for 5 minutes on a medium heat, before adding the roasted bones to the pan, and then sweat it down for a few more minutes
● Add the pastis, and reduce. Then add the fish stock and the white peppercorns, fennel seeds and bay leaves and bring the pan to the boil. Skim the top using a ladle
● Simmer for 30 minutes
● Pass through a chinois using a muslin cloth, ensuring that you press the stock to get all of the flavour
● Bring back to the boil and reduce by half. Then add the cream and reduce until sauce is thicker. Season to taste

Assembly

Plate the risotto and add the Cornish red mullet on top. Garnish as seen here in the picture.

Chef's Recommended Wine:

Nielson by Byron, Santa Barbara County Chardonnay, California, USA, 2014

Fillet of Cured Wild River Tweed Sea Trout, Sea Herbs, Samphire & Pickled Cucumber

Serves: 4

Ingredients:

Trout and Cure

1 side of line caught River Tweed wild sea trout
250g salt
250g sugar
1 star anise
100g lemon zest
5g whole white peppercorns
100g lovage leaf and stalks

Method:

● In a food processor, add all of the ingredients for the cure and blitz together. Place the fish on a flat tray using greaseproof paper and cover the sides of fish with the cure
● Massage the cure into both sides and cover with a second sheet of greaseproof before using a second weighted tray on top to press it together. Refrigerate overnight
● The following day, wash off the cure under cold water. Pat both sides down using a cloth to rid of any excess water to ensure that they are as dry as possible
● If you are using the fish during the next week, wrap the pieces in greaseproof paper to keep dry
● If you wish to preserve the fish for longer, we would recommend that you either store the portions in food bags or vacuum pack them

Onion Crisp

Feuille de Bric pastry
Free range egg yolk
Tsp onion seeds

Method:

● Separate one sheet of the pastry. Lightly egg wash the pastry using a brush and a lightly beaten egg. Sprinkle the top with the onion seeds and place on a baking tray.
● Bake in the oven on 190 degrees for 2-3 minutes, (ensure that the fan is switched off).
● When removed from the oven, leave on a cooling rack to cool down, and break it into shards ready for garnishing the dish. This will add some savoury notes as well as some crunch to our lovely salad.

Lovage Oil

100g blanched lovage leaf
150g extra virgin olive oil
150g sunflower oil

Method:

● First, we need to blanch the lovage leaves. To this add the remaining leaves and oils, and liquidise using a hand blender before passing through a muslin cloth
● This will create a beautifully clear lovage scented oil to be able to make our lovely lovage emulsion

Lovage Emulsion

2 egg yolks
1 tsp Dijon mustard
1 tbsp cider vinegar
Seasoning

Method:

● In a food processor, add the egg yolks, mustard, and vinegar
● Using a jug, gradually add the pre-prepared lovage oil until it thickens and continue to add until you reach the desired consistency
● Be careful not to split the sauce. Taste before you add the seasoning but keep in mind that our sea trout has already been cured and therefore has a salty taste
● We must always be conscious of achieving a balance throughout a dish

Salad

Oyster leaf and flower
Samphire
Sea purslane
Bronze fennel
Pickled cucumber (peeled, deseeded cubes of cucumber in a good quality Chardonnay vinegar and seasoning)

● Pick and wash all of the various leaves and sea herbs, ensuring that they are fresh

Assembly

Arrange salad around the cubes of sea trout, and shards of the onion crisp, before finishing with the lovage emulsion.

Chef's Recommended Wine:

Avondale, Jonty's Ducks, Pekin White, Paarl, South Africa, 2015

Roast Courgettes with Curthwaite Goat's Curd & Tempura Courgette Flower

Serves: 4

Ingredients:

Deep Fried Courgette Flower

1 female baby courgette flower (Peter Jones Wirral Watercress)
1 yellow courgette cut into four cylinders
100g Curthwaite goat's curd
1 egg yolk
50g finely grated Grana Pedano cheese
1 sprig of thyme
Chopped chives

Method:

- In a bowl, mix together the goat's curd, parmesan, egg yolk, stripped thyme, chopped chives and lemon zest, creating the filling
- Using a Parisienne baller, scoop out the centre of the courgettes. Drizzle them with olive oil, season, and put these on a flat baking tray with parchment paper. Put them in the oven on 180degrees for 3- 4 minutes
- Add the filling to a piping bag with a nozzle, and pipe it into the centre
- Put them back into the oven on 200degrees for 3-4 minutes, ready to serve

Espelette / Tempura Batter

20-25cl Wenlock Spring sparkling mineral water
Maldon sea salt to taste
Tsp fish seasoning (see glossary)
Tsp lemon zest
100-150g plain flour - Sifted
2 ltr sunflower/vegetable oil for deep frying (Total Produce)
Flour for dusting the courgette flowers

Method:

- Mix the sieved plain flour by hand with salt, fish seasoning and lemon zest
- Add the mineral water little by little to get the correct consistency and leave it to rest for 15 minutes
- Heat the oil to 170 degrees
- Dip the flowers in the flour and then dip it in the batter and fry until golden brown, turning to ensure consistency of colour
- Season, and drain on a blue cloth to rid of any grease

Black Olive Tapanade

80g black olives, pitted and marinated in Herbes de Provence
25g extra virgin olive oil
2 cloves of garlic - peeled
1 lemon - squeezed
10g fresh basil leaf
10g fresh flat leaf parsley
(Anchovies can be added to this if you would prefer)

Method:

- Add all ingredients to a food blender, gradually adding extra virgin olive oil, creating a texture worthy of a quenelle

Aubergine Puree

Turbot stock (please see the glossary)
1 tsp Dijon mustard
Butter to finish
Fish seasoning (please see the glossary)

Salad - Marinated Herritage Tomatoes

1 punnet of herritage tomatoes
Pea shoots
Hooton watercress
Frisse
2 branches of mint - picked leaves and chopped
2 branches of flat leaf parsley - picked leaves and chopped
1 tbsp extra virgin olive oil
Black pepper and Maldon sea salt to season

Method:

- We use seasonal leaves that give different flavours, textures and preferably colours. This will give the salad an extra depth, both visually and to taste. In this case we have used pea shoots for sweetness, watercress for a pepper taste, frisse for bitterness, and parsley and mint leaves to finish
- A drizzle of 8-year-old aged Balsamic Vinegar

Assembly

Create different layers of flavours and texture by applying a base of the aubergine puree in the centre with some decorative drags on the plate. Then we add the marinated tomatoes, the deep-fried courgette flower, and the quinellaed tapenade. The stuffed baked courgettes are then added, before finishing with a beautifully dressed salad and some edible flowers.

Chef's Recommended Wine:

Domaine de la Vielle tour Rose, Cote de Provence, France, 2016

Summer Memories with Marjorie

Serves: 4

Ingredients:

Hebridean hogget
Loin, rump, shoulder, sweetbreads
Charred leek
Golden beetroot washed, peeled and blanched in saffron and vegetable stock
British broad beans
British broad bean flowers & tendrils
Flat leaf parsley, mint, chives, fennel seed, Maldon salt,
Cracked black pepper
Orange juice and zest
Vegetable stock (to blanche the pearl barley) 50% reduced vegetable stock
Vegetable oil
Premium unsalted butter
Braised pearl barley (blanched in vegetable stock for 20 minutes and allowed to cool naturally)
Hay from your local farm shop
Carrot and orange puree (see method and quantities below)
Lavender
Black olive tapenade
Anchovy fillet
Rosemary

Pearl Barley

Celery finely diced
Banana shallots finely diced
Leek washed finely diced
Mint freshly picked and chopped
Carrots washed peeled and finely diced
Chives
Fresh flat leaf parsley
Orange zest & juice

Method:

● Braise in white lamb stock for 17-20 minutes, allow to cool on a tray naturally and set aside
● Finely diced carrot, shallot, celery, leek, orange zest
● Add fresh parsley, fresh mint and fresh chives just prior to serving
● Add lamb stock and jus during the re-heating process (barley can absorb liquids quite quickly)

Hay roast hogget rump

Hay
Rosemary sprigs (Art School Herb Garden)
Lavender sprigs (Art School Herb Garden)
Lamb seasoning (See Glossary)

Method:

● Seal the seasoned rump of hogget and add to a pan of hay, lavender, rosemary
● Ignite the hay, extinguish and place the lid on
● Roast in the oven for 9 mins at 165 degrees, then remove and allow to rest for a further 5 minutes before carving

Pan roast loin of Hogget

Method:

● Heat a thick bottomed cast iron pan and use sunflower oil to seal the seasoned barrel of Hebridean hogget
● Finish with unsalted butter and cook for 3-4 minutes
● Allow to rest for 5 minutes before flashing to carve

Confit pressed shoulder of Hogget

This element of the dish is in keeping with the ethos of utilising all cuts from the nose to tail of the hogget. To successfully incorporate the confit pressed shoulder in to the dish it would have to be prepared in advance (Tuesday is our preparation day in the restaurant) due to the length of roasting and pressing time as detailed below. The cooking liquor created through this process is used to enhance the overall quality of the jus.

Method:

● We start with the shoulder on the bone, with just the knuckle and the rack bone from the opposite side removed
● This joint is sealed all of the way around and seasoned with the special Art School seasoning
● The joint is placed in a roasting tin approximately 4-5 inches deep with root vegetables (carrot, celery, onion, leek, rosemary, garlic, bay, leaf, peppercorn)
● This is covered with 3-4 pints of 50% reduced stock - we use True Foods - just enough to cover the shoulder and root vegetables
● The dish is filmed and foiled and placed into the oven at 160-170 degrees for 3½ to 4 hours
● Remove and allow to cool. Pass the stock, taking out all of the herbs and root vegetables. The stock is reduced, skimming any excess fat this is then added to the jus process as detailed below
● The joint is allowed to cool. The meat is taken off the bone, removing excess fat and any sinew and other impurities
● A small amount of the jus is added back to the meat, with butter and chopped chives, mint and parsley
● The meat is pressed overnight between two weighted gastronorm trays, creating a pressed confit terrine of lamb.
● On the day of the course the terrine is sliced in a rectangle and passed through the oven. This becomes the centre of the dish

● Continues over

- Continued from previous

Seasoned flour for the sweetbreads

50g plain flour sieved
to taste
¼ tspn ground cumin
¼ tspn ground coriander
Pinch of Maldon salt
Pinch white pepper

Method:

- Blanch in cold salted water, bring to the boil for 5-10minutes let them sit.
- Refresh in cold water and then peel (remove the membrane as this can be very tough).
- Dry then dust in the seasoned flour and pan-fry until golden brown.

Puree

3 large carrots, washed, peeled and chopped evenly

Tspn light Muscovado sugar
Juice of ½ orange
50g unsalted butter
Muslin bag with ½ tspn fennel seeds and orange zest
100ml vegetable stock (50% reduced - True-foods)
Seasoning to taste

Method:

● Cook until soft and drain off any excess liquor
● Puree in a Thermomix or with a stick blender
● Adjust the seasoning and texture before serving with butter, white pepper and salt.
● The puree should be silky smooth and suitable for dotting and plate design, as pictured.

Jus

50% reduced lamb stock from True-Foods
25g redcurrant jelly
25ml Port

Sprigs of thyme and rosemary

Method:

● Heat lamb stock and add port, redcurrant jelly and herbs.
● Reduce to drizzling consistency and whisk in cold butter to finish before passing through a sieve to remove the herb stalks ready to serve.

Assembly

Each component should be treated with respect and to enjoy this 10/10 meal as it should be, plate as pictured above.

Chef's Recommended Wine:

Valenciso Reserva, Rioja, Spain 2010

Peterhead Turbot with Native Lobster, Lime and Mango salad and Mousseline potatoes

Serves: 4

Ingredients:

Peterhead Turbot

1 prime Peterhead turbot - the larger fish give a better yield and the chunky fillets work best for this dish. You can ask your fishmonger to fillet and skin but do retain the head and bones for an amazing stock

Lobster

1 Native lobster

Salad dressing

40ml Olive oil
25ml white wine
1 lime juice and zest
Salt
White Pepper

Method:

- Blend all the ingredients for the salad dressing with a hand blender and place in a bottle ready to serve

Pomme Mousseline

150g potatoes
150g butter
60ml double cream
¼ nutmeg
Pinch of salt
Pinch of white pepper

Method:

- Wash, peel and boil the potatoes in seasoned water until cooked. Drain and place back in the pan to dry out
- Now, in the Thermomix, add the potatoes, butter and double cream and blend until smooth. Don't over blend. Add the salt, pepper and nutmeg to season

Spinach

100g spinach
10g butter
Salt

- Wilt in a hot pan with the butter and add the salt to taste

Salad

1 lobster claw meat
4 red chicory leaves

Frisée
Watercress
Oyster leaf
Bronze fennel
Mango cubes and puree

Method:

- Place the frisse, watercress, oyster leaf and bronzed fennel in a bowl and using the dressing, lightly coat the leaves. In a separate bowl, season claw meat with the same dressing and start to build the salad on the place using all the ingredients

Beetroot pickle

3 baby beetroot
50ml vinegar
20ml water
10g sugar

Method:

- Thinly slice the beetroots using a mandolin, Use a small round cutter and cut each slice with it. Mix the water, vinegar and sugar togther and add the beetroot to it

Bisque

1 lobster shell
4 plum tomatoes
1 fennel
1 white onion
3 garlic cloves
200ml tomato juice
300ml water
200ml cream
125g butter
25ml Martell cognac

Method:

- Roast the empty lobster shells in the oven for 20 minutes on 180 degrees. Sweat all the vegetables and add the bones to the pan. Then add the water and tomato juice and leave to reduce by half. Now blend with the bones in
- Pass the stock through a fine chinois and pour back into the pan. Add the butter cream and cognac and leave to reduce by half again until it's a sauce consistency

Assembly

Dress with sturgeon caviar and a lobster medallion.

Chef's Recommended Wine:

Charles Heidsieck, Blanc Des Millénaires, Champagne France 1995

Pan-roast Fillet of Peterhead Hake, Pomme Mousseline & Southport Potted Shrimp

Serves: 4

Ingredients:

Hake

4 portions of hake fillet, approximately 150-200g per portion
Our espelette fish seasoning (see glossary)
Maldon sea salt

Method:

- Preheat the pan until smoke-point, season the hake skin side with Maldon sea salt and flesh side with fish seasoning and place skin side down on the pan with vegetable oil for 1 minute to 1 minute 30 seconds
- Place under the grill or in the oven for 2-3 minutes on a medium to high heat
- Add a knob of butter to baste and turn the fish.
- Serve when cooked (slightly translucent)

Pommes Mousseline

4-5 Large Potatoes Cyprus & Jersey Royals (Seasonal for spring, washed, peeled and diced)
50ml Double Cream
50g Unsalted Butter
Maldon salt and ground white pepper to taste
Grated nutmeg (not pre-ground)

Method:

- Cut potatoes into small cubes, cover with boiling water and butter and simmer for 6-8 minutes until potatoes are cooked through
- Strain and place them back in to the pan to remove the moisture
- Gradually add some cream and butter and mix with a hand blender until smooth. Season to taste
- Keep warm ready for plating with a cartouche on top

Sauce

2 pots of potted shrimp including the butter (Southport potted)
1 beef tomato cut in to concasse
1 shallot peeled and diced
50g Lilliput capers in white wine vinegar
30g freshly chopped chives
30g freshly chopped parsley
Lemon zest julienne of 1 lemon
Sunflower cress and oyster leaf to garnish

Method:

- Finely dice the shallots and the diced, deseeded and skinned tomato and add to a pan. Add the chopped parsley, chives and lemon zest and gently heat adding the butter, potted shrimp and capers
- Keep warm ready for plating.

Spinach and Ramson Leaf

200g Baby leaf or Spinach
100g Ramson leaf and preferably wild garlic flower heads to garnish

Method:

- Baste the spinach and ramson leaf with butter and oil and sweat for 1 minute on a high heat, drain on a kitchen cloth before plating.

Assembly

Make a pond of mousseline potato using the back of your spoon to make a circle. Then layer the sapphire and wild garlic as a bed for the fish. Finish with the southport potted shrimp and caper butter, three wrapped onions and garnish with sunflower cress and a little oyster leaf.

Chef's Recommended Wine:

Domaine Brocard Sainte Claire Chablis, Burgundy, 2015

Asian Marinated Tofu, Spaghetti Vegetables, Baby Spinach, Girolle Mushrooms & Pak Choi Shoots

Serves: 4

Ingredients:

Asian Marinade (a little bit of Singapore)

Kikkoman Soy Sauce
50g Fresh Root Ginger, Peeled and Roughly Chopped
50g Garlic, Peeled and Roughly Chopped
1 Red Chilli
The Zest and Juice of 1 Lime
50g Fresh Corriander, Leaf and Stalk

Method:

● To make the luxurious Asian Marinade, add all of the ingredients to a bowl and mix together until combined, using a stick blender. To this the Tofu will be added

Tofu

Tofu, 120g per portion (our preference is to use a product called seacakes. We use this because it has strands of seaweed running through it and gives the tofu an added texture and depth of flavour. If you can't get your hands on this, then you can use plain tofu made from bean curd only).
1 large courgette
1 large carrot
20 medium sized girolle mushrooms, brushed and trimmed
150g baby leaf spinach, washed
Almonds, 5 per portion
10ml vegetable oil
50g sesame oil
Maldon salt

Method:

● Allowing five cubes of tofu per person, each diced at 2cm cubed, place into the bowl of marinade, only using half of it
● The remainder of the marinade will be used for the sauce to garnish. Leave the tofu to absorb the marinade in the fridge for at least 1 hour

● Remove the tofu from the marinade. Place the cubes onto a non- stick tray or a tray with parchment paper, and place into the oven on 200 degrees for 3- 4 minutes until they are hot and slightly coloured
● Do not overcook otherwise the tofu will dry out. If you prefer, flash frying is also a good way to cook the dish
● With a spiraliser or a Japanese vegetable turning cutter, create some vegetable spaghetti. Add that to a hot pan and toss in a little vegetable oil, leaving a slight bite and texture
● Finish it with a splash of marinade
● Using a little bit of sesame oil, sweat down the baby spinach and finish with a little soy sauce, which will be absorbed into the leaf

Beetroot Puree

Please see the glossary page

Garnish

Bok Choi
Sunflower cress

Assembly

To create the finished plate, centre the spinach garnishing the Tofu around it. Add your spaghetti vegetables on the top.
Dot the beetroot puree and roasted almonds around the dish, drizzling your marinade around the plate.
Complete using by using Bok Choi and sunflower cress for decoration.

Chef's Recommended Wine:

Edouard Leiber Gewurztraminer Hatschbourg Grand Cru, Alsace 2014

Passion Fruit Delice

Serves: 10

Ingredients:

Genoise Sponge

2 eggs
60g sugar
60g plain flour

Method:

● Whisk the eggs and sugar together to a ribbon stage and then sift the flour in. Fold in carefully to knock out any unwanted air
● Spread on a flat black Gastro with the silicone mat on top and bake for 5 minutes on 180 degrees until light golden brown. Take out and leave to cool
● Line 2 small trays with cling film. Cut out the shape of the tins on the sponges and place the sponges in the tins

Filling

150ml water
75g sugar
1 ltr cream
550g white chocolate
2 passion fruits (scooped)
4 bronze leaf gelatine leafs

Method:

● Leave the gelatine in cold water to soften. Meanwhile heat up the water and sugar in a pan and when the gelatine has softened, add it to the mix to melt. Bring to the boil and pour over the chocolate to melt it
● Whisk the cream until it reaches soft peaks. Don't over-whisk. Fold into the cooled-down white chocolate mix. Pour the mix over the sponges

Topping (for one delice)

250g (frozen puree) passion fruit boiron
50g sugar
2 gelatine leaves

Method:

● Soften the gelat Foam

150g Passion Fruit Puree
0.7g Xanthan Gum
0.7g Sosa Whip (Hy Foamer)

Method:

● Place all the ingredients in the mixer, then using the whisk attachment, whisk to form a foam. Place in the piping bag

Sorbet (you will need two Paco Jet beakers)

1 pineapple cut into small cubes
700g mango puree
300g sugar
100g trimoline

Method:

● Melt the mango puree, Trimoline and sugar together in a pan and pour over the diced pineapple cubes in the beaker. Freeze to -22 degrees. Emulsify to order in the Paco jet (please note traditional ice cream and sorbet makers can be used to churn but make the ice cream the day before to allow it to set properly)

White Chocolate Crumb

200g white chocolate

Method:

● Bake the white chocolate on 180 degrees for 3 minutes to a light golden brown. Leave to cool and then blend in the Thermomix

Assembly

Portion the delice and place on the plate as shown in the picture
Pipe the passionfruit foam and raspberry puree onto the plate. Pipe some raspberry puree where the white chocolate crumb goes and place the crumb on the top so the sorbet doesn't slide on the plate
Make a white chocolate curl by melting the chocolate and draping it on greaseproof paper over a rolling pin then place on top of the delice and scoop the sorbet on the crumb then serve

Chef's Recommended Wine:

Marchesy di grey L'Altro Moscato 2009 Piemonte Italy

Fresh Lime Tart with Earl Grey Sorbet and Caramel Chouquette

Serves: 12

Ingredients:

Sweet Pastry

100g unsalted butter
200g plain flour (sieved)
500g caster sugar
1 free range egg

Method:

● Place butter and flour in the kitchen bowl with the paddle mix and start on the lowest setting. Meanwhile, mix the egg and sugar together
● Once the flour mix is at a breadcrumb stage, slowly add the egg mix until combined. Stop the mixer, take the pastry out and wrap in cling film. Rest it in the fridge for 1 hour
● When rested, roll out the pastry in between 2 greaseproof sheets to 3mm thickness. Place in the desired tin and bake for 10 minutes on 180 degrees
● Once cooked, leave to cool on a rack. Remove pastry and line the tin with cling film. Place the pastry back into the tin.

Lime Curd

10 limes
400g caster sugar
5 free range eggs
3 egg yolks
200g butter

Method:

● Zest and juice all the limes and place them in the Thermomix bowl. Add all the other ingredients into the bowl and place on speed 2.5 on 85 degrees for 10 minutes
● When cooked, pour the mix into the tin over the pastry through a fine chinois and set for 5 hours in the fridge

Choux Buns

50g unsalted butter
60g caster sugar
60g plain flour

Method:

● Mix all ingredients together until you form a dough. Roll in between two sheets of greaseproof to 2mm and leave in the fridge for 30 minutes to set

Raspberry Puree

100g raspberries

Method:

● Blend the raspberries to form a puree.

Choux Pastry

120g milk
56g unsalted butter
1.5g sugar
1.5g salt
65g plain flour
120g whole eggs

Method:

● Place the butter, milk, sugar and salt in a pan and bring to the boil. Add the flour and leave to cook until the mix comes off the side of the pan. Place mix in a Kitchen Aid bowl with the paddle attachment on medium low setting and leave in there to cool down slightly
● Whisk the eggs together and on a medium speed slowly add egg mix to the dough until it has a dropping consistency
● Place the mixture into a piping bag and pipe out onto a lined flat tray. Cut out the pastry using a circular cutter and place on top of each choux bun
● Bake in the oven for 25 minutes at 160 degrees until golden brown. Take out and leave to cool down on a rack
● Place in an airtight container ready to serve

● Continues over

- Continued from previous

Caramel chocolate filling

275g Blonde Orelys Chocolate
500g whipped double cream
75ml water
37g caster sugar
2 bronze leaf gelatine leafs

Method:

- Place the gelatine in cold water to soften. Once softened, take out and put in a pan with the water and sugar. Bring to

the boil and pour over the chocolate through a sieve
- Mix together and then fold in the whipped double cream. Pour into a tub and leave to set in the fridge. Place in a piping bag ready for service.

Earl Grey sorbet

30g Earl Grey tea
550ml water
150g caster sugar
60g glucose
60g Pro sorbet

Method:

- Place all the ingredients in a pan and bring to the boil. Take off and place a lid on top
- Let the mix infuse for 30 minutes and then pass through a fine chinois
- Place in a Paco Jet beaker to freeze for 24 hours at -22 degrees. Place in the Paco just before service

White Chocolate Crumb

200g white chocolate

Method:

- Bake for 5 minutes until a light golden brown
- Let it cool down and then blitz lightly. (Do not over blend)

Assembly

Plate as above with apple marigold and begonia flower garnish.

Chef's Recommended Wine:

Paparazzi Prosecco Di Valdobbiadene, Itlay NV

Coconut Ice Cream, Chickpea Meringue, Rum Roasted Pineapple & Pineapple Gel

Serves: 24

Ingredients:

Pineapples

100ml of rum
1 whole orange - zest and juice
1 whole lime - zest and juice
1 whole lemon -zest and juice
50g brown sugar

Method:

- In a tub, place the sugar, rum and citrus elements. Cut and peel the pineapple, ensuring that you remove the core, and cut it into cubes
- Add the pineapple into the rum mix and leave it in the fridge overnight to infuse
- When you are ready to serve, place the pineapple pieces on a tray in the oven at 180 degrees for 5 minutes to warm through
- Remove from the oven and using a blow torch, char the pineapples

Vegan Meringue

100g chickpea juice
100g sugar

Method:

- First you need to line a flat baking tray with baking parchment.
- Using a Kitchen Aid, whisk the chickpea juice using the whisk attachment until it doubles in size and is light and fluffy.
- Slowly add in the sugar and keep whisking until it forms stiff peaks. Place the meringue in a piping bag with a plain nozzle and pipe the meringue into circles onto the baking tray.
- Dehydrate the meringues in the oven for 8 hours on 65 degrees.

Vegan coconut ice cream

400ml coconut milk
100g sugar
Pinch of salt
1 vanilla pod
40g Pro sorbet

Method:

- For the ice cream, place all of the ingredients into a Paco beaker and freeze to -22 degrees. Pacotize until it is needed.

Coconut Puree

200ml coconut milk
10g sugar
2g agar agar

Method:

- Place the agar agar, sugar and coconut milk in a pan and bring to the boil
- Pour into a tub to cool down, and once the mix has cooled down and gone hard, blend it using a food processor until it is smooth. Place it into a piping bag

Toasted Seeds

20g linseeds
20g sesame seeds
20g poppy seeds
20g sunflower seeds
20g chai seeds

Method:

- Place all of the seeds in a bowl and mix them together. Spread them out on a tray and place them in the oven for 5 minutes on 180 degrees
- Take them out, and let them cool down, before leaving them in a tub ready for serving

Assembly

To serve this dish, place the seeds in the centre with the meringue disc on top. Ball the ice cream into a scoop and place this on top of the meringue. Decorate the plate with pineapple around the ice-cream and dot the puree around the plate to finish as per our photograph.

Chef's Recommended Wine:

Montes, Late Harvest gewürztraminer, Colchagua, Chile 2013

Autumn

Warm Salad of Herdwick Lamb's Tongue, Butcher's Wife Black Pudding & Autumn Leaves

Serves: 4

Ingredients:

Herdwick lamb's tongue

4 Herdwick lamb's tongues
Mirepoix vegetables - garlic, carrot, celery, onion, leek
Bouquet garni
2l lamb's stock (see glossary)

Method:

- To slow braise the lamb's tongue, place the bouquet garni, mirepoix vegetables and the lamb's tongue into a saucepan and cover with lamb's stock (See glossary)
- Cover the deep roasting tray with cling film then foil and put in the oven for 3 hours at 170 degrees
- Once cooked, allow them to cool and then remove the outer skin whilst they are still warm. Once they have been peeled and chilled, slice the lamb's tongue. Each tongue will allow for between three and five slices
- We recommend that three slices per portion will be a substantial amount for a starter

Raspberry Emulsion

Raspberry puree
5g poppy seeds
Tsp honey
50ml olive oil
50ml vegetable oil
1 egg yolk
10ml raspberry vinegar
Tsp mustard

Method:

- For the raspberry emulsion, place one egg yolk in a bowl. Add 10ml of raspberry vinegar, and one tsp of mustard and combine
- Whisk in the olive oil and vegetable oil to thicken and add the honey and raspberry puree. Then add the poppy seeds to the mix
- When the mixture is done put it into a small plastic bottle and leave in it in the fridge

Pickled Girolles

12 small girolles, brushed and trimmed
Pickle liquor (25g sugar, 25g salt, 20ml white wine vinegar, sprig of thyme, 5 black peppercorns, 200ml water)

Method:

- Pickle the Girolle mushrooms in pickle liquor

For Plating

1 head frisse
Parsley leaf
Mint leaf
Watercress
1 banana shallot
4 slices of Edge's Butcher's Wife black pudding
12 Raspberries
50ml Natural Jus

Method:

- Make a salad in a bowl using frisse, watercress, parsley and mint leaves with sliced shallot
- Dot the raspberry emulsion around the plate, pan fry the black pudding and the lamb's tongue to add colour and finish it with butter
- Char the fresh raspberries with a torch

Assembly

Place the charred raspberries around the plate. Place the black pudding in the middle and then the salad. Add the slices of lamb's tongue on top and the girolles around the salad. Finish by pouring the natural jus on top.

Chef's Recommended Wine:

Bodegas Luis Canas, Crianza, Rioja, Spain, 2013

Confit of Autumn Rabbit Pie with Pickled Vegetables & Piccalilli Vinaigrette

Serves: 4

Ingredients:

Rabbit pie

1 whole rabbit - skinned and gutted
Separate into the saddle and remove and trim the loins ready to cook. Put the shoulders and legs to one side ready to be cooked in duck fat
500ml duck fat
2 cloves garlic
2 sprigs of rosemary
4 peppercorns
1 bay leaf
Rabbit/chicken stock (please see the glossary)
Pre-rolled sheet of butter puff pastry
1 egg yolk

Method:

● In a pan or a skillet, colour each side of the front legs and back legs before placing them into the duck fat with the herbs, and cooking them on a low heat until tender for about 1 hour to 1 ½ hours dependant on the size of you rabbit
● This should be placed into the oven on 150 degrees

Polenta Pastry

400g plain sifted flour
200g polenta (we add a portion of polenta to this recipe to add an extra bite and texture as there are a lot of soft elements within this dish).
2 sprigs of thyme, stripping the leaves
300g unsalted Butter

Method:

● Add all of the ingredients into a large bowl, and rub through the cold butter until it has reached a sand-like texture
● Bring it together using ice cold water. Be careful not to overwork your pastry otherwise it will crumble. Wrap this in clingfilm and allow it to rest in the fridge for at least an hour before you roll it out
● Remove the pastry from the fridge, and allow it to come back to room temperature before working it
● Roll the pastry out onto a floured surface using a rolling pin, to about 3mm thick. This is now ready to be placed into your desired pastry cases
● Any shape of pastry case can be used for this, but at The Art School we chose to use small round cases. These are baked blind in the oven on 160 degrees for 10 minutes. These can then be left to one side to cool down

Piccalilli

1 cauliflower
3 large onions
8 large shallots
1 cucumber
600ml white wine or cider vinegar
300ml white malt vinegar
1/4 tsp chopped dried red chilli
350g caster sugar
50g English mustard powder
25g ground turmeric
3 tbsp cornflour
Salt and pepper

Method:

● Cut the cauliflower into small florettes. Chop the onions and shallots into 1cm dice and add them to the bowl of prepared cauliflower florettes
● Peel and de-seed the cucumber and cut it into 1cm dice. Sprinkle the cucumber with a little salt and leave for a quarter of an hour to draw out some of the moisture. Rinse the cucumber under cold water and leave it to dry. Then add this to the other vegetables
● Put the vinegars into a pan, and add the chilli before bringing it to the boil. Take it off the heat and leave it to stand for thirty minutes. You don't want to pour this over your vegetables as they will start to cook
● Strain and discard the chilli
● When the vinegar is cool, mix all of the dry ingredients in a bowl and add a little of the vinegar and mix it until it has formed a thin paste. Bring the rest of the vinegar back to the boil and pour it into the sugar/spice paste and stir it well
● Stir it well until it is mixed together with no lumps. Return it to the pan and simmer for about three minutes. Pour over the vegetables and mix it well
● Store them in a sterilised jar such as a mason jar. Then store them in a cool place. You will be able to keep this for a month or two

Pickled Vegetable Garnish

Carrot, ¼ cm cubed, pre- blanched
Cocktail gherkins, (cornichons), halved
Radish, finely sliced on a mandolin
Baby Onions, Pre- Blanched, Quartered,
2 tbsp mirin, (Japanese corn syrup)
2 tbsp rice wine vinegar
Pinch of salt
Pinch cracked black pepper

- Continued from previous

Method:

- Add all of the above ingredients into a bowl, and toss them together. Leave for 30 minutes before serving

Sauce

2 pints of natural chicken jus

Stock made from the rabbit saddle bones
50ml double cream

Method:

- Add the chicken stock to a pan, and to this place in the rabbit bones
- Cook for an hour before passing through a muslin cloth

- Reduce this down, and finish with the double cream
- Adjust the seasoning, and this produces a sauce which we affectionately call a Cafe Au Late

Garnish

Chervil
Pink begonia and nasturtium watercress flowers

Assembly

Present as per our photograph

Chef's Recommended Wine:

Joseph Cattin, Pinot Noir (Lightly Chilled), Alsace, France, 2014

Fillet of Turbot with Cucumber Tagliatelle, Palourde Clams, Cockles & Keta Caviar

Serves: 4

Ingredients:

Fillet of turbot:

4 portions of turbot, 125g per portion. De-boned and skinned - ideally from the chunky part of the fillet. Ask your fishmonger for the fillets from a larger fish
1 X 2kg Wild Scottish turbot – filleted (Wards Fish, Birkenhead Market with bones supplied)
Maldon salt to taste

Method:

● Skin, trim and portion the turbot fillet and ensure that the fillets are dry before pan-frying
● Pan-fry the seasoned turbot in vegetable oil, finish with butter
● Drain onto kitchen cloth ready to serve

Cockles and Clams

Cockles and Palourde clams, 200g of each. Ensure that these are washed and checked thoroughly before use.
½ lemon
2 cloves of garlic, peel and finely chopped
1 banana shallot, peeled and finely chopped
1 sprig of thyme, leaves stripped

Method:

● Sweat off the garlic, parsley stalks, shallot, and include a strip of thyme leaves, in a knob of butter adding a squeeze of lemon
● Then add your cockles and clams, and steam until the shells start to open
● Don't overcook them otherwise they will look dry. Strain the juice from this and add it to your sauce to retain all of the flavour from both the clams and the turbot
● Pick the meat from the shells and leave it on the side

Vegetable Garnish

2 medium sized cucumbers, peeled and sliced into ribbons using a mandolin or peeler
½ lemon
Fresh dill

Method:

● In a saute pan, add the cucumbers to a little bit of butter. This will give a lovely bit of colour, and it will drive off any excess water
● We still, however, want to retain the texture of the cucumber. Remove from the pan and drain off onto a cloth on a flat tray
● Garnish the centre of your serving plate using these ribbons, and coating them in a little of the sauce

Sauce

Turbot stock (please see the glossary)
1 tsp Dijon mustard
Butter to finish
Fish seasoning (please see the glossary)

Method:

● The fish sauce comes from the cooking liquor of the cockles and clams. That, in itself, is a derivative of the original turbot stock. Therefore, we complete a full circle and bring the dish together using all the elements of the dish
● Reduce the past stock and cooking liquor. Finish with the mustard and butter, and season to taste
● Check the consistency of the sauce. You don't want the cucumber's water content to thin it down

Garnish

Kata caviar (salmon roe)
Fresh dill/fennel tips
Sunflower cress

Assembly

Plate the turbot on a bed of the cucumber ribbons, adding sauce, cockles, clams and vegetables plus garnish.

Chef's Recommended Wine:

Poderi Colla, Riesling, Langhe, Italy, 2015

Breast of Red Leg Partridge, Puy Lentils, Smoked Southport Pork Loin, Leeks & Pear

Serves: 4

Ingredients:

Breast of Partridge

2 whole red leg partridge (breasts for pan frying, legs for stocks and sauces)

Method:

- Season your breasts using the game seasoning (See glossary)
- In a hot pan, add the breasts skin side down to add some colour to the presentation side
- This is a very small bird so it is crucial that you do not overcook the meat
- It is imperative that it retains its natural juices. It will take a minute cooking on either side to gain a rosie centre
- Pay extra care to ensure there are no lead shot and feathers

Lentils

Southport smoked pork loin lardon 1cm cubed, blanched and ready for cooking
120g puy lentils, washed, blanched and cooled ready for use
Brunoise of vegetables (carrot, leek, celery, parsley, stripped thyme)
1 medium leek, sliced into discs. Blanch in vegetable stock, drain and dry ready to be charred

Method:

- In a hot pan, add the lardons until they are crisp. Remove from the pan and leave on a tray to rid of any excess fat
- Leave the fat from the lardons in the pan, and add to this the brunoise of vegetables and sweat them down
- Add the lardons back into this pan to finish it off by tossing it through with the lentils

Sauce

Natural jus (please see glossary)
500ml pear cider

Method:

- Add 500ml pear cider to natural jus and reduce to a syrup

Caramelised Pears

1 pear - peeled and diced
Caster sugar/water to make a caramel
25ml Calvados

Method:

- Using a saucepan, add the sugar covering it with your water
- Boil it until it reaches the point where it looks like it is going to start to caramelise
- At this point add the Calvados and the diced pears, being careful not to burn yourself as this will flambé as the alcohol burns off

Assembly

Plate as shown in the picture. Add a garnish of fennel and caramelised pears. Carve the partridge horizontal through the breast and open to show a slightly rosey and juicy finish.

Chef's Recommended Wine

Calisari Pinot Noir, Romania, 2016

149

Veal Cutlet, Shin and Marrow Bone with Girolles, Parsley Root & Heritage Carrots

Serves: 4

Ingredients:

Gisburn Farm Milk-fed Veal

We are keen supporters of English veal production because we wish to help change of perception of a product which had previously been challenged over perceived animal welfare issues.
Marrowbone
Shin of veal
French trimmed cutlet

Marrowbone Butter

30g Marrowbone, extracted from the marrowbone which we have cut down the centre creating a "canoe" type shape. This can be prepared by your local butcher.
100g unsalted Butter
10g tarragon leaves
Pinch of Maldon sea salt
Pinch of pepper

Method:

● Add all of the ingredients together and blend in a food processor
● Don't over process it, you just want to combine them together otherwise it will split
● Roll it out into a cylinder shape onto parchment paper, and wrap it in clingfilm
● Chill this in the fridge until you require it

Shin (Osso Bucco)

Veal sock (see the glossary)
125ml white wine
25g tarragon
25g thyme
½ bulb of garlic
25g parsley stalks
Peppercorns
1 bay leaf
300g mirepoix vegetables, including leeks, carrots, onion and celery
Method:

● Seal the shin in a pan before adding it to a roasting tin and allowing a level of veal stock to just cover the meat
● Put it in the oven covered with foil, and cook it on 150 degrees for 2- 2 ½ hours
● Remove the meat and leave it to rest before cooking the garnish in the lovely juices as per the recipe below

Cutlet

1 cutlet per person
50g cooked shin veal to be placed back into the marrowbone
1 quenelle of marrowbone butter
Veal seasoning (please see glossary)

Method:

● Ask your butcher to give you a French-trimmed rack of veal. This is a beautiful cut of meat which I adore
● From this rack, you will get 6 nice portions, and a spare chef's treat. Brush a little vegetable oil over the veal, and season the cutlet
● Place on the grill, 2 minutes on either side to give it some lovely markings and a charred flavouring
● Remove the meat and leave it to rest before cooking the garnish in the lovely juices as per the recipe below

Garnish

¼ baby cabbage
Parsley root puree
Heritage carrot
Sauce

Method:

● The carrot and baby cabbage can be cooked in the veal stock as a similar idea to a pot au feu
● We then retain the flavour of the cabbage and the carrot, ready for the final reduced sauce

Assembly

For the plating of this dish, you can see from our photograph that we place the canoe-shaped marrowbone, filled with the pulled shin meat, in the centre of the dish
We build the vegetable garnish around the carved cutlet and parsley root puree before finishing with the marrowbone butter, and our shin
The pot au feu style sauce is the last thing to garnish the plate. The sauce is a reduction of the cooking liquor passed through a sieve and muslin then seasoned ready for use

Chef's Recommended Wine:

Vallet Freres Meursault, Burgundy, 2014

Liverpool Bay Seabass, Sauce of Palourde Clams, Celeriac Puree and Rainbow Chard

Serves: 4

Ingredients:

Sea Bass

4 line-caught Liverpool Bay seabass - 200g per steak

This fish is the most important local fish within our region. This is why we like to treat it with the upmost respect. It is a beautiful and rare ingredient and the quotas for line-caught fishing will decrease until we can sort out sustainability within our waters.

Method:

- Using a hot pan, place your seabass fillets skin-side down using sea salt only on the skin
- After 3 minutes finish the cooking process by cooking it through for 1- 2 minutes under the grill, adding a knob of butter to the pan, and turn over the fish to complete
- This will give the skin a nice golden and crispy texture

Sauce

3 Palourde clams, per person
100ml fish stock (please see the glossary)
1 clove of garlic, roughly chopped
Parsley - including the stalks
½ lemon juices
10g unsalted butter

Method:

- Sweat off the garlic and parsley in a nob of butter adding a squeeze of lemon. Add your clams and steam until the shells start to open. Don't overcook otherwise they will look dry
- Strain the juice from this and add it to your sauce to retain all of the flavour from both the clams and the seabass
- Pick the meat from the shells and leave it on the side
- Clean three of the shells, per portion, and add the meat back into these. Sprinkle a little herb breadcrumb over the top and grill to gain a little colour

Celeriac Puree

1 medium celeriac - washed, peeled and diced
200ml whole milk
50g unsalted butter
Pinch of ground white pepper
Pinch of Maldon sea salt
50ml vegetable stock

Method:

- Put the celeriac into a pan and cover them using the milk, butter and vegetable stock
- Bring to a simmer and cook them until they are soft
- Add the drained celeriac to the liquidiser, (ensuring that you retain the liquor to adjust the consistency as required), and blend until smooth
- Adjust the seasoning to taste
- Put the puree into a plastic squirty bottle or piping bag ready to serve

Fish Stock

100ml fish stock (please see the glossary)and cooking liquor from the clams to ensure that all of the flavours are captured
50ml double cream
25g unsalted butter
100ml dry vermouth
Seasoning to adjust

Method:

- Bring the stock and cooking liquor to a boil before reducing to a simmer
- Add the cream and whisk in the butter. Finish the sauce by adding the vermouth, and season to taste

Vegetable Garnish

Rainbow chard
Romanesco florettes

Method:

- For the Rainbow Chard, wash and trim then chiffonade the leaf
- Trim and blanch the Romanesco Florettes, then reheat in a little vegetable stock
- Drain onto a cloth on a tray to rid of any excess liquid

Assembly

To plate this dish, centre the purees with the vegetable garnish on top. The fish then sits directly on top of this, with the clams scattered around the side. This dish is then finish with a "swooshing" of sauce.

Chef's Recommended Wine:

Lucien Crochet, La Croix du Roy, Sancerre, 2015

Pan-roast Fillet of Peterhead Hake with a Risotto of Filey Crab

Serves: 4

Ingredients:

Sherry Vinegar Reduction

50ml sherry vinegar
350ml red wine
1 sprig of thyme
1 bay leaf
1 clove
20g muscavado sugar

Method:

- In a pan, pour the sherry vinegar, red wine, thyme, bay leaf clove and the sugar
- Bring this to the boil and reduce by half until the mixture becomes thick enough to drizzle on the plate
- Pass this through a sieve and leave it to cool
- When cool, whisk in a little olive oil to emulsify
- Put this to one side ready to dress your plate

Risotto

280g of Aborio rice
500ml of fish stock (see glossary)
1 onion - Finely Diced
1 clove of garlic - thinly chopped
1 bunch of chives - finely chopped
1g Cheshire saffron
20g mascarpone
10g butter
100ml white wine
100g white Filey crab meat
Brunoise of vegetables - 1 carrot, 1 leek and 1 stick of celery

Method:

- For the risotto, heat up the stock with saffron, and then sweat down the onion, brunoise and the garlic using a knob of butter until they are soft
- Add the white wine and reduce.
- Gradually add the stock, until the risotto is cooked.
- Finish with mascarpone, chives and crab meat. Season to taste.

Hake

4 portions of chunky hake fillet – around 150g per portion
50ml extra virgin olive oil
Art School fish seasoning (see glossary)
Knob of butter
1 link of morcilla

Method:

- Heat a frying pan to smoking point, and add olive oil
- Season the fish using The Art School Fish Seasoning (See glossary), and put in the pan skin side down using a splash of olive oil and a knob of butter
- Once the fish starts colouring, finish with the morcilla in the oven for 3 minutes
- Add the butter to the pan and let it foam until it becomes nutty, and then baste fish with butter and the juices of morcilla

Assembly

To plate this dish, we arrange the saffron risotto in the centre of the dish. On top of this, add the morcilla, finishing with showcasing the fish directly on top. For this dish, we have used some charred onions for garnish. However, you can use any vegetables of your preference that are in season.

Chef's Recommended Wine:

Telmo Rodriguez, Basa, Rueda, Spain, 2016

Guanaja Dark Chocolate Mille Feuille

Serves: 24

Ingredients:

Pastry

1 sheet of butter puff pastry

Method:

- Place the sheet of puff pastry in between two flat trays and bake for 13 minutes at 180 degrees. Check to see if it's golden brown. Cut the pastry to the desired size. Keep small pastry sheets in an airtight container ready for service

Chocolate Mousse Filling

195g whole milk
60g egg yolk
35g caster sugar
237g 55% dark chocolate
380g 35% semi-whipped double cream

Method:

- Heat up the milk to boiling point. Whisk the eggs and sugar together then pour 1/3rd of the milk into the eggs Pour that back into the pan, place back on the heat and bring to 83 degrees while stirring constantly
- Pour the mix over the chocolate through a sieve to melt the chocolate. Let the chocolate mix cool down to 40 degrees then fold in the semi-whipped cream. Leave to set in the fridge. When ready place into piping bag ready to serve

White Chocolate Snow

112g 33% white chocolate
84g tapioca maltodextrine

- Melt the chocolate over a Bain Marie. Place the tapioca in the Thermomix and start on speed 4 while pouring in the melted chocolate. Make sure it's blended well. Take out and place in an airtight tub ready to serve

Guanaja Chocolate Cremeux

250g whole milk
250g double cream
100g egg yolk
50g caster sugar
240g 70% Guanaja dark chocolate

Method:

- Heat up the milk to boiling point. Whisk the eggs and sugar together then pour 1/3rd of the milk into the eggs. Pour that back into the pan. Place back on the heat and bring to 83 degrees while stirring constantly.
- Pour the mix over the chocolate through a sieve to melt the chocolate. Once melted mix together and place into an airtight tub to set in the fridge.

Assembly

Serve as in the photograph, garnish with the pineberries and Mexican marigold. Be careful not to overfill the layers with the chocolate mousse keeping it nice and neat for presentation. ideally build the Mille Feuille on the plate and garnish around the main element.

Chef's Recommended Wine:

Mas De Lavail, Maury Expression, France 2014

Ormskirk Damson Sorbet with Granny Smith Apples & White Chocolate Soil

Serves: 36*

Ingredients:

Crumble

100g plain flour
100g caster sugar
100g unsalted butter
100g natural oats

Method:

- Mix all the ingredients together in the mixer with the paddle attatchment until its all evenly mixed, then bake at 180 degrees until golden brown
- Leave to cool down then break up and place in an airtight container ready for service

Apple Cubes

1 discovery apple
1 lemon
200 ml water

Method:

- Cut the apple into small cubes and place in the water, squeeze all the juice of the lemon in the water and leave ready for service

Damson Sorbet

650ml damson syrup
65g Pro sorbet

*This will make a batch when the damsons are in season. Pop the remainder in the freezer for future use
Method:

- Blend the two ingredients in the Thermomix for 2 minutes on full speed.
- Pour into a Paco beaker and freeze for 24 hours at -22 degrees.
- An alternative is to use a traditional sorbet or ice cream machine.

Damson Syrup

1000g de-stoned damsons
500g sugar (adjust depending on acidity of damsons)
300ml water

Method:

- Place all the ingredients in a pan and bring to the boil, simmer on a medium heat until the damsons are very soft
- Pass the mix through a chinois leaving the damsons in the chinois and making a syrup
- Blend the damsons together to make a puree, adding more sugar if needed

Assembly

Plate the dish as shown and drizzle the syrup over.

Chef's Recommended Wine:

Charles Heidsieck Rose Reserva, Champagne, France Non-vintage

Pavlova of Gin-soaked Blackberries, Turkish Delight Ice Cream & White Chocolate Soil

Serves: 4

Ingredients:

Turkish Delight Ice Cream
(Makes a litre of ice cream. Store the rest for later use)

500ml whole milk
150 ml double cream
130g caster sugar
10ml rosewater
pink food colouring
85g egg yolks

Method:

- Heat up the milk and cream in a pan and bring to the boil
- Whisk the egg yolks and the sugar in a bowl and then add the milk to the egg and back to the pan
- Bring the mix up to 83 degrees and then add the rosewater and food colouring. Pour into the Paco beaker and freeze for 24 hours at -22 degrees

Meringue

100g sugar
100g egg whites

Method:

- Whisk the egg whites in a mixer until light and fluffy then all the sugar slowly, until stiff
- Spread out on greaseproof and then dehydrate for 6 hours on 65 degrees. When ready break into shards for garnish keeping some as little ski slopes to house the crumb and ice cream

White chocolate crumb

100g white chocolate chips

Method:

- Place on a baking tray, evenly spread out and bake on 180 degrees for 4 minutes until golden brown, leave to chill and then break up and then blend into a crumb.

Gin blackberries

100g blackberries
100ml gin

Method:

- Place blackberries in the gin and leave to marinade for at least 2 hours.

Pear and Grape Jam

400g grapes
6 pears
200g sugar
250g blackberries
200ml water

Method:

- Place all ingredients in a pan and bring to the boil, reduce on a medium heat for 30 minutes until everything is very soft.
- Take out and blend in the thermo until smooth, pass through a chinois and place in a piping bag ready for service.

White Chocolate Snow

84g tapioca maltodextrine
112g white chocolate

Method:

- Melt the white chocolate and then put the tapioca in the Thermomix and turn onto a slow to medium speed, pour the chocolate in while mixing.
- Take out and then place into an airtight container ready for service.

Assembly

Plate this dish as seen in the picture.

Chef's Recommended Wine:

Gorka Izagirre Late Harvest Txakoli, Bizkaiko Txakolina, Spain, 2013

Winter

Seared King Scallop with Butcher's Wife Black Pudding & Romanesco Cous Cous

Serves: 4

Ingredients

Scallops and Black Pudding:

4 diver caught king scallop in the shell (ask your local fishmonger to prepare them if you prefer)
4 Edge's Butcher's Wife black pudding cut into rounds the same size as the scallops that you're working with same size as the scallops that you're working with
1 Granny Smith apple

Method:

- To prepare the scallops in the shell, we remove the medallion from the shell. We move the roe and the frill ensuring that all the membranes are removed
- At this stage place the medallions onto a blue jay-cloth to draw out moisture content before cooking. This is extremely important to ensure the perfect cooking of your scallop
- Don't use frozen or tubs of scallops for this reason. It is all about the integrity of the ingredients you are using
- Using a cast iron heavy bottomed frying pan, heat on a high temperature to almost smoking but not burning. Using a splash of oil, add the scallops to the pan
- Season the scallop on the presentation side using Maldon salt only. This would be the side that was connected to the flat part of the shell, not connected to the foot of the scallop where the rounded part of the shell is. On the foot of the scallop sprinkle a little of the fish seasoning. At the same time as cooking the scallops, add the black pudding to the pan
- Sear the scallops for a minute until they are golden brown, before carefully turning them over and adding a knob of butter. Turn the black pudding at the same time
- Cook for another 30-seconds-to-a-minute maximum to ensure that your perfect scallop is of a translucent colour through the centre
- Don't overcook the scallop. When they are cooked, removed them from the pan and place onto a cloth to rid of any excess grease
- Cut the Granny Smith apple into sticks, with a squeeze of lemon over the top to avoid discolouring

Puree

120g golden raisins (pre-soaked in the dessert wine and white wine vinegar for 30 minutes)
1 banana shallot, peeled and finely diced
1 clove peeled garlic
50ml dessert wine
10ml white wine vinegar
Maldon salt

Ground white pepper to taste
Method:

- In a large pan, sweat off the shallots and garlic on a medium heat, using a splash of vegetable oil and a knob of butter
- Add to the pan, the soaked raisins, and bring to the boil
- Simmer for 2-3 minutes, until the raisins are soft, and then blend them down to a puree using a hand blender
- Season to taste

Romanesco Cous Cous

1/3 head Romanesco - grated/food processed
½ lemon - squeezed
20g chopped chives
Seasoning
Splash of natural jus (see the glossary page)
Fish seasoning (see the glossary page)
Bok choi shoots for garnish

Method:

- In the food processor, add the Romanesco and blitz to a chunky breadcrumb consistency. Add a squeeze of fresh lemon juice, the chopped chives, and season to taste. Mix together and place in the fridge until ready to use
- Using the remainder of the Romanesco, blanch the remaining florettes in a pan of boiling salted water to two minutes. Then remove placing directly into iced water to stop the cooking process
- Drain the florettes on kitchen cloth to rid of any excess water. Cut lengthways down each florettete to create a flat surface
- When all elements are ready to be plated, add the florettes to a hot cast iron pan with a splash of oil to char the surface
- Finish with a knob of butter and use to garnish the final dish

Assembly

Lay the romanseco cous cous, golden raised puree and scallops as shown in the photograph. The Granny Smith apple sticks are used to finish the final plate adding acidity and balance to the final dish along with the crisp earthy flavour of the baby Bok Choi shoots.

Chef's Recommended Wine:

Macia Batle Blanc de Blancs, Mallorca, Spain, 2016

Baked Salsify, Parmesan Crust, Roast Navet & Sour Cherry Dressing

Serves: 4

Ingredients:

Salsify

2 sticks of medium sized salsify thoroughly washed and peeled. Place immediately into cold water with lemon juice to avoid oxidisation
4 sheets Feuille de Bric (This can be substituted for filo pastry)
100g finely grated parmesan
1 egg yolk to glaze the Feuille de Bric
25g onion seeds

Method:

● Remove the salsify from the cold water, and place straight into a pan of salted lemon water, and bring to the boil. Allow to simmer until tender
● This will take approximately 4-6 minutes, dependent on the thickness of your salsify. Once this is tender, remove from the pan and place straight into iced water. This will stop the cooking process immediately
● Remove from the water, and pat dry using a cloth to rid of any excess water
● Take your pastry and egg wash the inside using a pastry brush and egg yolk. Sprinkle a healthy amount of finely grated parmesan over the top, finishing with seasoning
● Roll the pastry tightly around the salsify stick before sealing it with egg wash. Brush the outside with some more egg wash and finish with the onion seeds for decoration and garnish
● Place this on some oiled parchment paper, or even better a silicone mat, placed onto a flat tray, and leave to chill in the fridge until you are ready to bake it
● When it comes to cooking the salsify, bake in the oven on 180 degrees for 5-7 minutes depending on the efficiency of the oven. Later, when plating up of this dish, nip the ends using a serrated carving knife to ensure that you don't break your pastry. This will showcase the salsify as you will be able to visually see it

Vegetables

4 baby leeks
8 florettes of Romanesco
2 baby onions
2 navet

Method:

● Wash and trim all of your vegetables, and blanche them in a pan of boiling water until tender
● Remove them from the pan, ensuring that they are dry. Finish them in a pan with a knob of butter and season to taste

Dressing

1 egg yolk
Maldon sea salt
Juice of half a lemon
Tsp Dijon mustard
100 ml extra virgin olive oil
Griottine cherries - 5 per plate, plus the juice retained for the dressing

Method:

● Place the egg yolk into a bowl, along with your salt, lemon juice and mustard
● Gradually, add in your oil and continuously whisk
● Finish your dressing by tossing through your cherries

Garnish

Red mustard frills

Parsnip Puree

Please see glossary page

Assembly

Finish the plate by garnishing with your florettes of Romanesco, and the parsnip puree as per our photograph. To bring all of the elements together, add your smooth dressing between your dots of puree.

Chef's Recommended Wine:

Podere Castorani, cadetto, Trebbiano D'Abruzzo, Italy, 2015

Senna Lane Farm Pork Belly, Cheek plus Southport smoked loin & Edges Butcher's Wife Black Pudding

Serves: 4

Ingredients:

Pork

4 * 50g square portions of saddleback pork belly, pressed and cooked
2 pork cheeks, halved per portion trimmed of all fat and sinew
4 * 25g loin of Southport smoked pork
4 * 25g squares of Butchers wife black pudding (optional)

Apple & Vanilla puree

2-3 Granny Smith apples peeled and diced
½ vanilla pod scraped (or 2 drops of vanilla essence)
50g caster sugar
25ml of apple juice
Squeeze of lemon juice

Method:

• Cook all of the ingredients together in a pan and then puree with a stick blender or place in a food processer to make a smooth puree. At the restaurant we use a Thermomix
• Place in a bottle and chill ready for service

Roasted Almonds

2 dozen almonds
splash of olive oil
pinch of Maldon salt

Method:

• Cover 2 dozen almonds with a splash of olive oil, a generous pinch of Maldon salt and place in a roasting tin and cook at 170 degrees until golden brown. Put aside for garnish

Pork Belly

4 celery sticks, washed and chopped
4 large washed, chopped and peeled carrots.
2 large onions, peeled and chopped.
1 large leek, washed and chopped mirepoix
3 bay leaves
10 peppercorns
10 parsley stalks
3 sprigs rosemary
1 medium garlic bulb, roughly cut
White stock 3l – see glossary
Organic Cider 500ml

Method:

• Place all of the ingredients including the liquor in a deep roasting tray, cling film and cover with foil. Cook for 3 hours at 160 degrees. You can use a water bath if you prefer, but I like the stock to make a sauce.
• After cooking, press the belly pork overnight in the fridge between two baking sheets. Portion into squares to go back in the oven for 3-4 minutes at 180 degrees. To finish the crackling, place the pork belly under a high heat grill or blow torch.

Cheeks

1 celery stick, washed and chopped
1 large washed, chopped and peeled carrot
1 large onion, peeled and chopped
1/3 large leek, washed and chopped mirepoix
1 bay leaf
3 peppercorns
3 parsley stalks
1 sprig rosemary
3 garlic cloves, roughly cut
White stock 3l (see glossary)
Organic Cider 500ml

Method:

• Seal the cheeks in a hot frying pan to caramelise before placing them in a deep roasting tray with the braising vegetables and liquor.
• Cling film and cover with foil and cook for 1 1/2hours at 160 degrees.
• Chill the pork cheeks overnight then portion ready to reheat in the Jus to serve.

Assembly

Combine the two cooking liquors, from the belly and cheek, and pass through a chinois and muslin. Reduce to a pouring syrup and season to taste.

Trim the pork smoked pork loin and butcher's wife black pudding to 25g square portions.
Pan fry separately in a little oil and butter. Plate and serve.

Garnish

3 Parsienne balls of fresh Granny Smith apples for garnish per plate, as photo
5 roast almonds per portion
Tablespoon of apple and vanilla puree
Broad bean flower and watercress to garnish

Chef's Recommended Wine:

Fromm La Strada Sauvignon Blanc, Marlborough, New Zealand 2015

Twice Baked Soufflé of Local Pink Tip Spinach & Mrs Kirkham's Lancashire Cheese

Serves: 4

Ingredients:

Twice baked soufflé

4 egg whites
50g plain flour, sifted
Generous knob of butter, plus additional for buttering moulds
400 ml whole milk
200g of spinach washed
1/4 leek finely chopped
1 bay leaf
1 strand of thyme
1 clove
½ onion
½ tsp of nutmeg

Method:

● First make a béchamel sauce. Melt a generous knob of butter in a large pan, and once melted add the flour and create a roux. Cook out the flour for a few minutes
● In another pan, pour your milk in with the thyme, nutmeg, onion, and clove, and bring it to the boil and leave it to infuse for 25 minutes
● Put the roux back on the heat and add the infused milk little by little until you reach a smooth mixture, and then pour it in to a tray. Cover with cling film and leave it to cool
● Prepare your moulds using the rest of the butter. Brush the melted butter into the moulds before dusting with some plain flour
● Cook the spinach and leeks in a pan with a splash of vegetable oil, add a knob of butter and season. Remove from the pan and place onto a cloth and leave them to cool
● Separate the eggs, and put egg white into a Kitchen Aid and whisk to soft peaks. Add a pinch of salt and a pinch of sugar and whisk until it reaches firm peaks
● In the meantime, place ½ of the béchamel mix in a bowl add gradually the egg yolk until it is mixed. Then mix 1/3 of the egg whites before folding in the rest
● Fill ½ of each mould with eggs mix, insert 1 dessert spoon of the spinach mix, and fill the mould with the egg mix on top so spinach is covered
● Cook in an oven for 12 minutes at 150 degrees, then drop temperature to 110 degrees for 10 minutes. Take it out and leave it to cool before removing them from the mould.

Leek and Mustard Sauce

1 celery stick, 2 leeks (keep the green on the top separate), 2 onions, 4 garlic cloves chopped
150ml of white wine
10 ml of cider vinegar
150ml of vegetable stock
10 fennel seeds, 5 black peppercorns, 1 bay leaf, 2 strands of thyme
250ml of cream
50g of butter

Method:

● Sweat down the vegetables in a splash of vegetable oil and add the butter until they soft. Add the cider vinegar and wine and then reduce it by half. Add the vegetable stock and the cream and bring to the boil, before simmering for 20 minutes
● Pass the sauce through a chinois.
● Reduce it down until it is thick and smooth. Season to taste
● To serve, put the soufflés in the oven for their second bake. These will take 3- 4 minutes on 185 degrees to rise and brown.

Assembly

Place a ladle of sauce in the middle of the bowl, with the soufflé straight from the oven directly on top. Finish by garnishing with a splash of extra virgin olive oil and some Hooton watercress.

Chef's Recommended Wine:

Pierre Bouree, Bourgogne Blanc, Burgundy 2016

Mr Ward's Loin of "Red Deer" Venison with Girolles, Black Truffle & Cavolo Nero

Serves: 4

Ingredients:

Venison

4 loins of venison, (150g tournedos). In the restaurant we would buy a saddle of highland red deer and trim it ourselves. However, you could ask your local butcher or game dealer to prepare it for you. (Ask for some bones so that you can make your sauce and stock).
Venison seasoning (see glossary)

Method:

- Heat a large cast iron/ thick bottomed saute pan on a high heat with a splash of vegetable oil until the oil is almost smoking but not burning
- Using the venison seasoning on our glossary page, sprinkle on all sides of the venison loin steak. Place these into the pan ensuring that each side is sealed and has a caramelised golden-brown colour. This should take about 2-3 minutes
- To the pan, add 50g of unsalted butter, cooking and basting for a further 2-3 minutes, coating the venison using a spoon
- Remove the loins from the pan, and rest them on a wire rack. Allow at least 10 minutes for the loins to rest, so that they retain their flavour and natural juices

Sauce

1ltr of venison stock
200ml of natural jus
Bouquet garni
10 juniper berries
50g of damson puree
100ml ruby port
50g of redcurrant jelly

Method:

- Reduce venison stock and natural jus with bouquet garni, and juniper berries by 2/3
- Then add the port, redcurrant jelly and damson puree, and reduce until the mix is a syrup-type consistency and can coat the back of a spoon
- Pass this through a chinois
- For an extra sheen and gloss, gradually whisk in a few cubes of unsalted butter
- By adding the butter gradually and not all at once it will ensure that your sauce won't split. "Monte au Beurre"

Venison Garnish

5 medium sized girolle and a handful of trompette mushrooms, brushed and trimmed
50g of truffle butter
2 sprigs of stripped thyme
Vegetable oil for frying
Cavolo nero - one head washed and trimmed
1 bunch of chives - finely chopped

Method:

- Prepare the Girolles mushrooms by peeling the stalks, and brushing off any forest debris
- Heat a pan with oil, and once heated add the mushrooms
- Fry them to give them some colour, then reduce the heat and add the butter and thyme. Cook for a further minute and season to taste
- For the Cavolo nero, remove the stalk/vein using a knife
- Cut the leaves into 10cm. Blanch for 30 seconds in a pan of boiling vegetable stock, and then pour it into a hot pan with a knob of butter and seasoning. Cook for a further minute until soft

• Continues over

- Continued from previous

Salted Baby Winter Potatoes

6 baby winter potatoes (ideally Pink Fir Apple Potatoes)
3 rosemary sprigs
250g rock salt
1tsp peppercorns
100g crème fraiche
20g finely grated Grana Padano
1tsp cream cheese,
1 egg yolk

1tsp horseradish
Parsley - 50g chopped leaves
50g panko breadcrumb
Venison seasoning

Method:

- Into a baking tray, add the potatoes and cover them with salt, rosemary and black peppercorn
- Roast them in the oven on 160 degrees for about 15-20

minutes, depending on the size of the potatoes
- Bake them until they are soft, checking them with
the tip of knife. Make a herb crumb by adding parsley
and breadcrumbs into a food processor, with the venison
seasoning and blend
- Remove the potatoes from the oven and leave to cool.
Once cool, cut the potatoes in half and trim the bottom round
edge, so it can sit flat on the plate
- Place these onto a flat tray, and pipe the mixture on top
Finish by sprinkling the parsley herb crumb on top

Assembly

Start to assemble the dish, and finish with the parsnip puree
(See glossary), to decorate as per the photograph. The timing
of the garnish items and the resting of the venison are the
crucible parts of the dish coming together.

Chef's Recommended Wine:

Ridge "Lytton Springs" Sonoma, USA 2012

Pave Rump of Salt Aged Lakeland Beef

Serves: 4

Ingredients:

Beef

150g, per portion, "pave" rump of salt aged Lakeland beef
from the Himalayan salt chamber
Beef seasoning (please see glossary)
2 sprigs of thyme
50g unsalted butter
25ml vegetable oil

Method:

- Coat all of the sides of the rump in the beef seasoning
- Using a hot, thick bottomed frying pan, heat it up to almost smoking point
- Using a splash of vegetable oil, add your rump to the pan, sealing all of the sides and edges of the meat
- Add your sprigs of thyme to the pan, and add a knob of butter. The butter will start to foam and gain a nutty taste
- Baste the meat using this for 3-4 minutes to guarantee it to be medium- rare, or rare if you would prefer

Vegetable Garnish

6 large Jerusalem artichokes, washed and blanched ready for
saute - allow 3 halves per portion
1 bunch of chives - finely chopped

Turnip

1 medium/large white turnip
250g unsalted butter
1 sprig of thyme
1 sprig of rosemary

Method:

- With the turnip, we want to create a fondant. We start by peeling and washing it, but cutting it into four even-sized discs
- In a hot pan, add your discs and allow some colour on either side
- Add an entire pack of butter, with the seasoning, a sprig of thyme and a sprig of rosemary, and roast in the oven on 160 degrees for 10- 12 minutes until they are golden brown and ready to use
- Check them as the cooking of these will vary dependant on the thickness of you discs

Artichoke Puree

Please see the glossary page

Caramelised Onions

Please see the glossary page

Natural Jus

Please see the glossary. Add and infuse for 20 minutes before serving after tarragon leaves.

Assembly

Start with a spoonful of caramelised onions. On top of this sits the three halves of artichoke, with your carved beef on the side of this. The turnip fondant sits to the side of this and finished with sporadic dots of puree. To finish, with your lovely tarragon infused natural jus.

Chef's Recommended Wine:

San Felice "Il Grigio" Chianti Classico Riserva, Tuscany, Italy, 2013

Roast Breast of Squab Pigeon with Beetroot Puree & Foie Gras

Serves: 4

Ingredients:

Squab

1 whole squab per person
Game seasoning, (See glossary)
4 tranches of foie gras - 25g per portion

Method:

- Start by removing the legs from the bird, these will be used for stocks and sauces. At this stage you will only be left with the breasts on the crown
- Place the crown, covered in some game seasoning, breast down into a hot-oiled pan. Seal the crown on all sides to ensure an even coloration. This now goes into the oven on 165 degrees for three minutes on each side depending on the size of the pigeon
- Remove from the oven, baste with some butter, and allow to rest for at least ten minutes to retain all of the natural juice. This is important because you have gone to the effort of leaving the meat of the bone before the carving and presentation of such a delight
- The foie gras requires a quick pan searing, 30 seconds either side for your final garnish

Squash

1 butternut squash - peeled and cut into 4 rectangular fondants
1 sprig of rosemary
1 sprig of thyme
250g unsalted butter
5 black peppercorns
3- 4 cloves of peeled garlic
Method:

- With the butternut squash, we want to create a fondant. We start by peeling and washing it, but cutting it into four evenly sized rectangles
- In a hot pan, add your portioned squash, and allow some colour on either side
- Add an entire pack of butter, with the seasoning, a sprig of thyme and a sprig of rosemary, and then leave them on a low heat to slowly cook through until they are golden brown and ready to use
- Check them as the cooking of these will vary depending on the thickness of your portions

Beetroot Puree

2 medium sized beetroots, seasoned in salt, roasted in foil
1 tbsp red wine vinegar
1 tbsp blackberry puree
50ml extra virgin olive oil

Method:

- Cook the beetroot in a small pan with water to cover, and cook until it is soft
- Peel the beetroot, cut the stem, and reduce the beetroot liquid by a 1/3. Keep this on the side
- Pour the beetroot into the food processor and start mixing. Add the beetroot juice and gradually pour in the olive oil until the mixture becomes smooth, and has gone a pink colour. Pass this through a sieve and season to taste
- Add to this your red wine vinegar blackberry puree to bring this all together

Hispi Cabbage

1 whole hispi cabbage - ¼ per portion

Method:

- Char each side of the cabbage on a plancha or on a thick bottomed hot sauce pan with vegetable oil. When charred finish with a label of vegetable stock and butter before draining and serving. Remember to season and brush with butter to finish

Garnish

Hooton watercress.

Assembly

Plate the dish as shown.

Chef's Recommended Wine:

Zolla Primitivo di Manduria, Puglia, Italy, 2015

Granny Smith Apple and Calvados Sponge with Vanilla Mascarpone, Candied Walnuts

Serves: 8

Ingredients:

Sponge Pudding

100g butter
100g sugar
100g self-raising flour
2 eggs

Method:

- To make the sponge, cream together the butter and sugar
- Slowly add the beaten eggs before folding in the sifted flour
- Pipe the mix into moulds and bake on 160 degrees for 13 minutes until they are golden brown
- Remove them from the oven and allow them to cool on a wire rack

Syrup

250ml apple juice
150g sugar
100ml Calvados

Method:

- While the sponges are cooking; add apple juice, calvados and sugar to a pan and reduce it by half to create syrup
- As soon as the sponge comes out, pour half of the syrup on to the sponge and leave it to soak

Crumble

50g oats
50g butter
50g plain flour
50g caster sugar

- Place the oats, butter, sugar and flour in to a bowl and mix them together to form a crumble
- Bake this mixture in the oven at 170 degrees until it is golden brown

Caramel Sauce

2 Granny Smith apples - peeled and balled
200g sugar
100ml water
80ml cream
6 chopped Granny Smith apples
1 vanilla pod

Method:

- Make a caramel by putting the 200g sugar and 50ml of water in a pan
- Once it reaches a dark brown colour, add the peeled and balled apples to the caramel before adding the cream
- Leave this to cook for 10 minutes on a low heat, before removing it
- Pour ¾ of the sauce into a pan, and place the apples in a separate tub ready for service
- In the pan which contains the toffee sauce, add the rest of the chopped apples and one vanilla pod
- Using 50ml of water, cook them until the apples are soft
- Blend this mixture using a hand whisk, and pass it through a chinois. Place it into a piping bag ready to serve

Candied Walnuts

50ml water
100g sugar
100g walnuts

Method:

- Place the 100g sugar and 50ml of water in a pan and bring to a soft ball, this is ideally 118 degrees
- Add the toasted walnuts and mix it until they are fully coated
- Remove them from the pan and place them in a tub ready to serve

Vanilla Mascarpone

100g mascarpone
50ml cream
15g icing sugar
1 vanilla pod - split and scrape into mascarpone

- Add the mascarpone, cream, icing sugar and vanilla to a bowl and whisk together
- This will then be quinellaed on top of the sponge during the plating up process

Assembly

On a baking tray, place a portion of the sponge in the oven. When it is hot, take it out, and start to plate up the dessert. As per our photograph, place the sponge in the centre of the dish, with the cream place on top. Garnish the plate with the apple place around the centred sponge and the sauce piped off centre.

Chef's Recommended Wine:

Donna Fuggata, Ben Rye, Passito di Pantelleria, Sicily, 2014

Sharing Plate, Includes: Pistachio Macaron, Chocolate Tart, Orange Delice & Choux Bun

Serves: 30

Ingredients:

Pistachio Macarons

150g ground almonds
150g icing sugar
150g caster sugar
1/4 tsp green colouring
55g egg whites for icing sugar
55g egg whites for caster sugar

Method:

● Place one lot of the egg whites in the Kitchen Aid, and attach the whisk attachment. Then put the caster sugar in a pan with enough water to dissolve it, and put it on the heat
● While that is heating up, sift the almonds and the icing sugar together
● Once sieved, put the other 110g egg whites into the mix. Don't mix it together yet. Once your sugar mix has come to 118 degrees, pour it into your whisked egg whites
● To make an Italian Meringue, while the machine is still whisking, mix your almond mix together to make a paste, and add your flavouring and colouring at this stage
● When the meringue mix is glossy and stiff, start adding it to the paste. Put 1/3 in first, then the next 1/3 mixing it thoroughly, making sure that there are no lumps
● Finally add the rest of the meringue and mix in again. To get smooth macarons you need to beat the mixture enough to make it runny, but don't over mix it
● Usually if you add the meringue in three stages it should be fine. Once it is all mixed, leave the mix to stand for 1 minute in the bowl. If it smooths out put it in a piping bag with a plain nozzle. If it is still grainy, beat with a spatula until it becomes smooth when left for 1 minute
● Let the macaroons skin over for a minimum of 20 minutes. If you lightly touch them and they don't stick, then they are ready. Don't leave them out for too long or they will lose their shine
● Pipe evenly onto a silicone mat and bake at 140 degrees for 13 minutes
● While they are in the oven, make your buttercream filling. See the recipe below. When the macarons are ready, leave them to cool down on a rack and remove from the tray as soon as they are cooled. Fill with flavoured butter cream and assemble. They are best served the day after

Pistachio Buttercream

200g butter
200g icing sugar
1tbsp pistachio paste

Method:

● Sieve the icing sugar into the Kitchen Aid and place all the other ingredients in with it, using the paddle
● Mix it on a high speed until light and fluffy, and take the mixture out and put it into a piping bag and pipe onto the macarons

Orange Delice – Sponge

120g sugar
4 eggs
120g plain flour

Method:

● In the mixing bowl, place the eggs and the sugar with the whisk attachment, and whisk into a ribbon stage (light and fluffy). Sift in the flour, and fold in gently trying not to knock the air out of the egg mixture
● Once all of the flour is incorporated, pour the mix onto a silicone mat on a baking tray and bake for 6 minutes at 180degrees. Take out and leave to cool
● Once cool, lift the mat off the tray, measure the size of the tin on the sponge and cut out the required amount of sponge. Place into a tin lined with cling film

Delise Filling

550g white chocolate
1 ltr of cream
5 gelatine leaves
75g sugar
150 ml water
1 orange zest

Method:

● Place the water, sugar and passion fruit seeds in a pan, whilst you leave your gelatine in water to soften
● Heat up the water mixture and dissolve the gelatine in it, and bring it to the boil
● When this is combined, pour it over the bowl of white chocolate, making sure that all of the liquid is on the chocolate, and leave it to settle and melt
● Don't mix it straight away or you will lose the heat from the liquid and the chocolate will not melt, so you will end up with a lumpy mixture
● In the Kitchen Aid add the cream with your whisk attachment, and whisk the cream until you reach a thick but not over-whipped cream

● Continues over

- Continued from previous

- Fold into your chocolate mix and then pour this mixture over the sponge. Make sure that the chocolate mix isn't too hot otherwise it will melt the cream. Leave it in the fridge to set

Orange Gel

250ml orange juice
2 gelatine leaves

Method:

- Soften your gelatine leaves in cold water
- Put the orange puree in a jug, and in a pan put 30ml of the puree to melt the gelatine
- Once it has melted, pour it back into the jug, and then pour it over the set white chocolate mousse
- Make sure the gel is not warm otherwise you will melt the mousse and you will have to start over

Choux Buns – Pastry Topping

50g butter
60g sugar
60g flour
Method:

- Mix all ingredients together until you reach a dough
- Roll in between two sheets of greaseproof paper to 2mm and leave it in the fridge for 30 minutes to set
- Cut out into circles, place on top of the piped choux buns

Choux Pastry

120g milk
56g butter
1.5g sugar
1.5g salt
65g flour
120g whole eggs

Method:

- Place the butter, milk, sugar, and salt in a pan and bring to the boil. Add the flour, and leave it to cook out until the mix comes off the side of the pan. Place the mix in the Kitchen Aid bowl with the paddle attachment and leave to cool slightly
- Whisk the eggs together, and on a medium speed slowly add the egg mix to the dough until it reaches a dropping consistency
- Place the mixture into a piping bag and pipe out onto a lined flat tray. Using a circular cutter, cut out the pasrty and place it on top of each choux bun
- Bake in the oven for 25minutes on 160degrees until golden brown. Take them out and leave them to cool down
Filling

75ml water
37g sugar
500 ltr cream
275g Blonde Orelys Chocolate
1 gelatine leaf

Method:

- Leave the gelatine in cold water to soften. Meanwhile heat up the water and the sugar in a pan, and melt the gelatine in it
- Bring it to the boil and pour over the chocolate to melt it
- Whisk the cream until it forms soft peaks, (don't over-whisk it), and fold it into the cooled down chocolate mix

Chocolate Tartlet – Sweet Pastry

200g butter
400g plain flour
2 eggs
100g sugar

Method:

- Place the plain flour and the cold diced butter in the mixer with the paddle attatchment, and mix together on a low speed until it has reached a breadcrumb stage
- The butter has to be cold otherwise this will form a paste and cannot be used. Mix the eggs and sugar together, and pour it into the flour mix, and again on a low speed mix it until it is just combined
- Remove the mixture and press it into a ball, wrap it in cling film, and place it in the fridge to chill and rest for 1 hour. Line the tartlet case mould with the butter spray and flour. Take the pastry out and press the tartlets into the mould
- Chill in the fridge and then bake on 180degrees for 9 minutes. Remove from oven and sand each tartlet case with a

microplain to a desired shape

Guanaja Chocolate Cremeux Filling

250g whole milk
250g double cream
100g egg yolk
50g caster sugar
240g 70% Guanaja dark chocolate

Method:

- Heat up the milk to boiling point. Whisk the eggs and sugar together. Pour 1/3rd of the milk onto the eggs, before returning this mixture back into the pan. Place it back on to the heat and bring to 83degrees while stirring constantly
- Pour the mix over the bowl of chocolate through a sieve to melt then mix together and leave it to set in the fridge

Assembly

Having prepared each individual treat, see the above for a serving suggestion.

Chef's Recommended Wine:

Domaine Grange Neuve, Monbazillac, France 2011

The End

The Art School Cellars

Our bespoke Champagne and wine cellar, The Art School Cellars, opened in September 2017. It's a delightful space where my team and I share our handpicked selection of premium Champagnes, fine wines, British cheeses and artisan Charcuterie. All can be enjoyed in an environment of comfort and relaxation.

Inspired by the Pinchos of the Basque Country and the Delis of Italy, we wish to encourage the culture of 'gastronomic grazing' in the hospitable city of Liverpool.

We have over 300 wines on offer and an extensive cocktail list coupled with fresh bread and small dishes available to order. All are prepared daily by The Art School Restaurant team.

As part of the exciting new addition to Liverpool, we also have our private Tasting Room. Suitable for up to ten guests, it provides a journey through matched foods and wines, whilst our Sommeliers are on hand giving detailed explanation for each pairing.

Our hope is that guests will enjoy our Liverpudlian warmth and friendliness while experiencing world-class food and drink consumption in sumptuous surroundings.

I wanted to expand on The Art School brand and the realisation that our lovely little restaurant bar was simply too small to accommodate all of our guests pre- and post-dining led to The Art School Cellars.

A bar like this is needed in our city – we needed a Champagne bar version of The Art School to continue the gastronomic journey and the food culture in the city.

The idea came about because of my love of travelling the world and discovering different cultures. For example, at Peck in Milan, every possible cheese, piece of Charcuterie, mushroom and dessert is on offer. It is just astonishing and their wine cellar is immaculate. Every level reminds you of the depth of culture and food knowledge and desire that there are in countries like Italy.

Then you go to the Basque Country, San Sebastian or Biarritz and there are little Pinchos on the bar that could win a Michelin star – as well as little glasses of wine. When you put the two together, the sun comes out, the clouds part and everything is wonderful.

For me then, The Art School Cellars are about trying to capture some of that and put it into an environment that offers hospitality in a Liverpudlian way. There are some marvellous tastes, like scallop with an Albariño, for example, which people will love.

Of course, finding the right person to turn my vision into a reality was key. It could only be an Italian or Spanish person, someone who has Charcuterie in their DNA because it's not ingrained into the British food culture.

It also required someone who is passionate about Mixology. That's where Gianfranco came in. I'll never forget his answer when I asked him about his favourite bar in London. I'd hoped he'd say either The Dorchester or the Ritz. Gianfranco said 'The Dorchester' so I was more than happy.

Just as I want the restaurant to be Le Gavroche of the North, I want the new bar to be the Dorchester or Ritz of the North. It should be international standard service with food, drinks, product knowledge and a great, welcoming environment. We want it to be an exemplar of what the Liverpool food and bar culture can be.

The Pinchos are basically miniatures of what we create in The Art School. This gives us the opportunity to demonstrate downstairs what we do up in the restaurant. We hope this will lead to guests trying the Tasting Room to sample them with five different wines and Pinchos or try the full Tasting Menu upstairs.

My aim downstairs is to give that experience to the guests, introducing them to different types of Pinchos and flavours of wine.

It is an interesting and sophisticated business and everything is in the right place to achieve out aims. We hope you'll find time to join us.

Glossary - Bread

Focaccia

900g Strong Flour, Sifted
400g Semolina
20g Salt
20g Sugar
800ml Water (Warm)
14g Yeast, Fresh
10g Fennel
10g Maldon Salt
20ml Olive Oil

Method:

- Place the semolina, flour, salt and sugar into a mixing bowl. Then, using a jug, add the lukewarm water and the yeast, and mix them together so that the yeast is dissolved.
- Add the water mix to the dry ingredients and mix it together. Knead the dough for 10 minutes until the dough is smooth.
- Place the dough in an oiled bowl and then leave it to prove, (ideally you want to leave it in an environment that's 27degrees), and allow the bread to prove until it doubles in size.
- Using some olive oil, grease the desired tray and make sure you grease up the sides too. Place the dough in the tray and spread it out so that the dough is evenly flat across the tin.
- Sprinkle the salt and fennel seeds evenly across the top of the dough.
- Then pour the olive oil over the top evenly, and then using the tips of your fingers press your fingers into the dough all over the surface.
- Again, place the dough in the prover, again to double in size, and then bake in the oven on 200degrees for 10 minutes until it is golden brown on top.
- Remove it from the oven and leave it to cool.

Pan Cerea

870g Strong Flour
180g Wholemeal Flour
100g Mixed Seeds
520g Milk
180g Water (Warm)
28g Yeast, Fresh
20g Salt
20g Sugar
3 Egg Yolks
20g mixed Seeds

Method:

- Pour the lukewarm water into a jug and add the yeast and milk and mix it all together.
- Place all of the other dry ingredients into the mixing bowl with the dough attachment, and pour the water into the bowl and knead it on a medium speed for 10 minutes until the dough is smooth.
- Place the dough into an oiled bowl and then place it into the prover until its doubled in size. The perfect environment for proving the dough is 27degrees.
- Remove the dough from the prover when it has reached this point and set up a tray lined with greaseproof.
- Using a bread scraper, cut the dough into 28g chunks and then roll them into balls. Place the balls onto the tray leaving at least 3cm in-between each ball, and then brush them with lightly beaten egg yolks using a pastry brush. Finish this part of the process by sprinkling the seeds on top.
- Place in the prover again and allow the dough to grow about a third of its current size, and then place them in the oven for 8 minutes on 200degrees.

Soda Bread

284g Buttermilk
150g Wholemeal Flour
150g Plain Flour, Sifted
8g Bicarbonate Soda
5g Salt
15g Rosemary (Blanched and Chopped)

Method:

- Preheat the oven to 400F/200C/Gas 6. Tip the flours, salt and bicarbonate of soda into a large mixing bowl and stir.
- Make a well in the centre and pour in the buttermilk, mixing quickly with a large fork to form a soft dough.
- Depending upon the absorbency of the flour, you may need to add a little milk if the dough seems too stiff, but it should not be too wet or too sticky.
- Turn the mixture out onto a lightly floured surface and knead the dough briefly.
- Form into a round shape and flatten the dough slightly before placing it on a lightly floured baking sheet.
- Cut a cross on the top of the dough and bake it for about 15 minutes on 200degrees.
- Remove from the oven and allow it to cool down.

Glossary - Stocks

Chicken Stock

Mirepoix: 5 carrots, 1 leek, 2 onions, 1 celery stick
5 kg of chicken bones
Bouquet garni
Fennel seeds, white peppercorns, bay leaves

Method:

- In a pan, pour in all of the bones, add vegetables and aromats and cover with water. Simmer for 4 hours
- Bring to the boil and skim off the scum from the top
- Once skimmed, simmer, and add all of the ingredients to the pan
- Simmer for 3 hours, continuing to skim off the scum throughout process
- Pass the stock through a muslin cloth into container

This stock can be kept for up to 5 days

Venison stock

Mirepoix: 5 carrots, 1 leek, 2 onions, 1 celery stick
5 kg of veal bones
Bouquet garni, 5 branches of rosemary
Fennel seeds, white peppercorns, bay leaves, 10 juniper Berries

Method:

- In a pan, pour in all of the bones, add vegetables and aromats and cover with water. Simmer for 4 hours
- Bring to the boil and skim off the scum from the top
- Once skimmed, simmer, and add all of the ingredients to the pan
- Simmer for 3 hours, continuing to skim off the scum throughout process
- Pass the stock through a muslin cloth into container
- This stock can be kept for up to 5 days

Fish Stock

Mirepoix: 5 Carrots, 1 Leek, 2 Onions, 1 Celery Stick
5 kg of Turbot or any other flat fish
Bouquet Garni
100g Parsley
Fennel Seeds, White Peppercorns, Bay Leaves
1 Lemon

Method:

- Wash the fish bones until the water runs clear, add vegetables and aromats and cover with water. Simmer for 4 hours
- Put the fish bones into a pan with all of the ingredients, and fill the pan with water until the bones are covered. Bring them to the boil and skim off the scum using a ladle. Simmer for 20 minutes, clearing of any scum
- Take off heat, and add the sliced lemon
- Pass through a muslin cloth
- This can be stored for up to 5 days

Turbot Fish Stock

1Kg turbot bones
½ lemon
Carrots washed peeled and cut into mirepoix
Celery washed peeled and cut into mirepoix
Whole black peppercorn
Bay leaf (Fresh)
1 large onion peeled and cut into mirepoix
Garlic bulb (1/2)
8 parsley stalks
Tspn fennel seed
3 sprigs fresh thyme
Cold water

Method:

- Classic fish stock preparation (As per above), or use True Foods fish stock 50% reduced

Beef stock

Mirepoix, 5 carrots, 1 leeks, 2 onions , 1 celery stick
5 kg of beef bones
Bouquet garni
10 fennel seeds
5 black peppercorns
Bay leaves
Rosemary

Method:

- In a pan pour all the bones, add vegetables and aromats and cover with water. Simmer for 4 hours
- Bring to the boil and skim the scum from the surface. Once skimmed, simmer and add all the ingredients to the pan
- Simmer for 3 hours. Continue skimming throughout the process
- Pass stock through a muslin cloth into container
- Can be kept for up 5 days

Lamb stock

Mirepoix, 5 carrots, 1 leeks, 2 onions , 1 celery stick, 1 fennel bulb
5kg of lamb bones
3 bulbs garlic, split
Bouquet garni
10 fennel seeds, 5 black peppercorns, bay leaves, rosemary, 3 gloves

Method:

- In a pan pour all the bones, add vegetables and aromats and cover with water. Simmer for 4 hours
- Bring to the boil and skim scum
- Once skimmed simmer and all ingredients to the pan and simmer for 5 hours, continue skimming throughout process
- Pass stock through a muslin cloth into container
- Can be kept for up 5 days

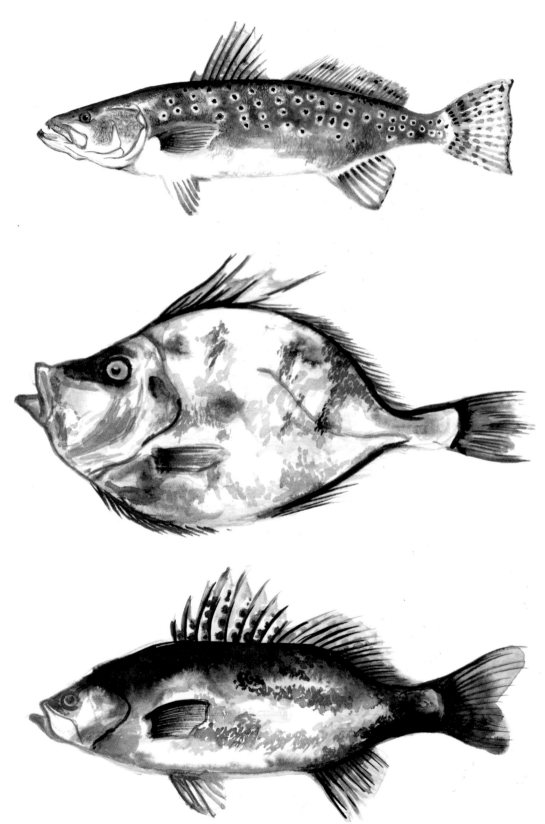

207

Glossary - Seasonings

Beef seasoning

200g maldon sea salt
2 sprigs of rosemary
4 sprigs of thyme leave stripped
10 fennel seeds
5 black peppercorns
1 bay leave
1 garlic clove peeled

Method:

● In a Robot Chef or spice mixer, blitz 150g of salt with all the ingredients until powdery. Pour in bowl and mix rest of the salt

Duck seasoning

200g Maldon sea salt
2 gloves and 1-star anis
1 sprig of rosemary leaves stripped
10 fennel seeds
5 black peppercorns
1 garlic glove
1 bay leaves and
1 dessert spoon of five spice
3 peels of orange

Method:

● In a Robot Chef or spice mixer, blitz 150g of salt with all the ingredients until powdery. Pour in bowl and mix rest of the salt.

Venison seasoning

200g Maldon sea salt
2 sprigs of rosemary leaves stripped
10 juniper berries, 5 fennelseeds, 5 black peppercorns
1 bay leaf
1 garlic clove peeled

Method:

● In the Robot coupe, blitz 150g of salt with the ingredients until it forms a powder like consistency, before pouring in a bowl and mixing with the remainder of the maldon salt.

Veal seasoning

200g Maldon sea salt
1 sprig of tarragon leaves stripped
1 branch of flat leaf parsley
10 fennel seeds
5 black peppercorns
1 bay leaf
1 garlic clove peeled
Zest of 1 lemon

Method:

● In the Robot coupe, blitz 150g of salt with the ingredients until it forms a powder like consistency, before pouring in a bowl and mixing with the remainder of the maldon salt

Fish seasoning

200g Maldon salt
½ teaspoon freshly ground white pepper
3 cloves garlic, peeled
1 teaspoon fennel seeds
1 teaspoon espelette pepper

Method:

● In a Robot Chef or spice mixer, blitz 150g of salt with all the ingredients until powdery. Pour in bowl and mix rest of the salt

Game seasoning

200g maldon sea salt
2 sprigs of rosemary leaves stripped
2 tsp thyme
10 red peppercorns
5 fennel seeds
5 black peppercorns
8 juniper berries
1 bay leave
1 garlic gloves

Method:

● In the robot, blitz 150g of salt with all the ingredients until powdery, pour in bowl and mix rest of the salt.

Chicken seasoning

200g Maldon sea salt
2 tsp thyme, 2 tsp tarragon, 2tsp parsley
10 fennel seeds, 5 white peppercorns, 1 glove
Peel of ½ lemon
1 bay leave
1 clove of garlic, peeled

Method:

● In the robot, blitz 150g of salt with all the ingredients until powdery, pour in bowl and mix rest of the salt.

Glossary - Puree

Roast cauliflower puree

1 cauliflower
300ml double cream
100ml milk
25g butter
Thyme
Bay leaves
2 garlic cloves
White pepper
Salt

Method:

- Roughly chop the cauliflower. Infuse the butter, milk and the cream with the thyme, garlic and bay leaves by bringing it to the boil and standing aside for 20 minutes
- Dry roast the cauliflower in the oven at 180 degrees until dark. Pass the liquid mixture into another pan and add the roasted cauliflower. Simmer until the cauliflower is soft
- Pass the cauliflower, and pour into the mixer and start to blend
- Gradually add the cream and mix until smooth.

Aubergine puree

4 aubergines
50ml olive oil
5 garlic cloves chopped
Maldon salt

Method:

- Cut the aubergines in half, score them, and brush over the olive oil. On the top, sprinkle with the garlic, and finish it with salt
- Roast the aubergines at 190 degrees in a roasting tray until they are soft and browned
- When they are cooked, pour all of the aubergines into the mixer and blend by gradually adding the olive oil until the mixture is smooth
- Pass the mixture and season to taste

Jerusalem artichoke puree

10 artichokes
10g butter
5ml of olive oil
250ml cream
5ml lemon juice

Method:

- Sweat artichokes in a pan with the oil and butter until they are soft and golden brown. Then add the cream and cook for a further 5 minutes to thicken the cream.
- Pour this into the mixer and blend. Finish by adding the lemon juice, pass and season to taste.

Parsnip puree

250g peeled and diced parsnips
200ml whole milk
50g unsalted butter
Pinch of ground white pepper
Pinch of sea salt
50ml vegetable stock

Method:

- Put the parsnips into a pan and cover them using the milk, butter and vegetable stock
- Bring to a simmer and cook them until they are soft
- Add the drained parsnips to the liquidiser, (ensuring that you retain the liquor to adjust the consistency as required), and blend until smooth
- Adjust the seasoning to taste
- Put the puree into a plastic squirty bottle or piping bag ready to serve

Beetroot puree

5 large beetroots
50ml of olive oil
2 strands of thyme
Maldon salt to season

Method:

- Peel the beetroot and cut into even dice. Pour diced beetroots into a pan of cold water add thyme, bring to boil and simmer until the beetroot are soft
- Once soft, drain, pour into a food processor, add seasoning and start blending
- Gradually pour olive oil into the mix until the puree is smooth. Pass through a fine chinois

Celeriac puree

2 celeriac
300ml double cream
100ml milk
2 strands of thyme to infuse
White pepper and salt

Method:

- Peel and dice the celeriac evenly. Put the celeriac in a pan, sweat for a few minutes without coloring then add thyme and liquid and bring to the boil
- Simmer until soft, check with the tip of a knife
- Then put the parsnip in a food processor and blend by adding liquid a bit at a time until the parsnip puree is smooth. Pass through a fine chinois. Season to taste

Golden raisin puree

300g golden raisins
2 shallots finely chopped
1 garlic glove
300 ml of wine
50 ml of sweet wine
10g butter
3g xanthan gum
White pepper and salt to taste

Method:

● Poor the golden raisins into a pan, cover with white wine and bring to the boil. Simmer until the raisin have rehydrated.
● Drain the raisins and keep the wine to one side. Put the wine liquid into a pan and reduce by 2/3s
● Add the chopped shallots and garlic into a pan with the golden raisins and sweat with a knob of butter until the shallots are soft(approx. 5mins)
● Add the sweet wine and the reduced wine. Bring to the boil then stand aside. Pour mix into the food processor and blend. Add 3g of xanthan gum to combine than pass through chinois. Season to taste

Burnt orange puree

4 oranges, cut into quarters
25g brown sugar
100g butter
50ml olive oil
100ml orange juice

Method:

● In a tray roast oranges with brown sugar in an oven at 180 degrees until the skin starts browning, then add the butter and cook for a couple of minutes
● Pour the mix into food processor and add the orange juice and olive oil. Pass through a sieve. If the mix is too thick whisk in more orange juice. Season

Rhubarb and beetroot puree

Ingredients:
4 rhubarb sticks,peeled, slow cooked in sections in the oven (sprinkle with sugar and a little water then cook until soft)
2 baby beetroots
50ml olive oil

Method:

● Cook the beetroot in a small pan with water to cover. Cook until soft. Cut the rhubarb into small chunks and cook in a pan with water until soft. That should only take a few minutes
● Peel the beetroot, cut the stem and reduce the beetroot liquid by 1/3. Keep to one side. Pour the beetroot and rhubarb into a food processor and start mixing. Add the beetroot juice and the cooked rhubarb. Gradually pour in olive oil until the mixture becomes smooth and has got pink colour. Pass and season to taste. Be careful to balance the seasoning and acidity

Glossary - Basics

Venison and damson jus

1l venison stock
200ml natural jus
Bouquet garni
10 juniper berries
50g of damson puree
100ml ruby port
50g of redcurrant jelly.

Method:

● Reduce venison stock and natural jus with bouquet garni and juniper berries by 2/3s
● Then add port, redcurrant jelly and damson puree and reduce until mix is syrupy and can coat the back of a spoon.
● Pass through chinois

Salt baked new potatoes

12 new potatoes
3 rosemary
250g rock salt
1tsp peppercorns
100g crème fraiche
1tsp cream cheese
1egg yolk
one tsp chives
1tsp horseradish
Leaves of one bunch of parsley
50g breadcrumb, and seasoning

Method:

● In a bowl pour creme fraiche, cream cheese, horseradish egg yolk and chives. Mix and season to the taste. Put in a piping bag
● For the baked new potatoes: cover the potatoes with salt on a tray with rosemary and black peppercorns. Roast until soft, check with tip of knife
● Make the herb crumb by adding parsley and breadcrumb into a Robot Chef until the mixture is fine and crummy. Season to taste
● Leave to cool. Once cool, cut in half and trim the edges so that it can sit flat on plate
● Pipe the mixture on top and sprinkle the parsley herb crumb on top

Twice bake soufflé

14 eggs
250g flour
300g butter
2l whole milk

1 bag of spinach washed
1/2 leek finely chopped
1 bay leave
1 strand of thyme
1 glove
½ onion
½ tsp of nutmeg

Method:

● First make béchamel, melt 250g of butter in a large pan, once melted add the flour and create a roux and cook flour out for a few minutes
● In another pan pour 2l of milk with thyme, nutmeg, onion, glove, bring to the boil and leave to infuse for 25 minutes
● Put roux back on the heat and add infuse milk bit by bit till you get a smooth mix, then pour in tray and cover with cling film and leave to cool
● Prepare mold with the rest of the butter.
● Brush melted butter in mold than dust with some plain flour
● Cook spinach and leeks in a pan with oil and a nob of butter and season, put on cloth and leave to cool
● Separate eggs, put egg white in kitchen aid and whisk one soft peaks add 15g salt and 20g sugars and whisk until firm picks
● In the meantime, place ½ of the béchamel mix in a bowl add gradually the egg yolk till mixed. Then mix 1/3 of the eggs white mixed until all mix, then fold the rest
● Than fill ½ of each mold with eggs mix, insert 1 dessert spoon of spinach mix, fold the egg mix on top so spinach is covered
● Cook in a oven for 12minutes at 150 degrees Celsius, than drop temperature to 110 degrees for 10 minutes. Take out and leave to cool before taking out of mold

Red cabbage

1 red cabbage
1 bramley apple
1 star anise
1 glove
10g five spice
100ml port
200ml red wine
50g brown sugar

Method:

● Cut the cabbage into quarters, remove most of the stem, then slice with a mandolin. Add cabbage to a pan then add the rest of ingredients. Sweat the cabbage until soft and the liquid becomes thicker and shiny. It will take around 25mins.

Natural Jus

Mirepoix: 10 carrots, 3 leeks, 5 onions, 3 celery sticks
10 kg of chicken bones
10 kg of beef bones
Bouquet garni
Fennel seeds
Black peppercorns
Bay leaves

Method:

- In a pan, pour in all of the bones and cover with water
- Bring to the boil and skim off any scum
- Once skimmed, simmer, and add all of the ingredients to the pan
- Simmer for 7 hours, continuing to skim throughout the process
- Pass the stock through a muslin cloth into another pan, then bring back to the boil and reduce until the jus is syrupy and coats the back of the spoon
- Pass through a muslin again and leave to cool in a container

Bisque Sauce

500g langoustine shells
Mirepoix of vegetables (3 carrots, 2 celery sticks, 3 onions, 1 bulb of fennel, 3 cloves of garlic)
Bouquet garni

200ml tomato juice
5g tomato puree
250ml cream
50ml cognac
5 white peppercorns
20g butter
4 plum tomatoes - chopped
½ lemon - sliced
10 fennel seeds

Method:

- Roast the shells in the oven for 30 minutes on 180degrees
- In a pan, sweat down the mirepoix for five minutes in a little bit of oil
- When the shells are ready to come out of the oven, add them to the pan with the tomato puree and sweat down furthermore. Add the cognac to the mixture and reduce this down
- Add the water and the tomato juice so that the shells and mirepoix are covered
- Add the bouquet garni, white peppercorns and the fennel seeds to the pan. Bring this to the boil and skim the top using a ladle, then simmer for thirty minutes
- Take this off the heat, add the slices of lemon, and then leave it to cool for five minutes. Pass through a chinois and muslin cloth into a smaller pan
- Reduce the stock by half, add the butter and the cream, and then reduce furthermore until the sauce can coat the back of a spoon

Glossary of Terminology, Caveats, Substitutes and How To Use This Book

- Temperatures – Temperatures are listed in degrees, which refer to Celsius.

- Desserts – We have provided accurate ingredients for the bulk quantities that we make in the restaurant, rather than portions to serve four. To cater for the number of guests that you are cooking for, simply divide the ingredients by the appropriate number. So, if for instance, the recipe indicates that a dessert will make 16 portions and you only wish to make four, divide by four to get the desired amount.

- Cooking times – These may vary for protein, depending on the size, thickness, quality, efficiency of your oven and so on. The temperatures and timings, therefore, should be used as a guide. The joy of cooking is in learning to use your senses of smell, taste and touch to judge the exact cooking time required.

The following are terms that some cooks may be unfamiliar with:

- Baine Marie – This is a water bath, or double boiler. It allows heat to be passed on gently and gradually to reach a fixed temperature, or to keep materials warm over a period of time.

- Bouquet Garni – Typically collected in a small piece of tied muslin, a bouquet garni is a collection of herbs that are used in stocks, soups, sauces and casseroles. It frequently comprises parsley, or their stalks, which impart bags of flavour, as well as thyme, a bay leaf and similar herbs. The small bag of herbs can be extracted when the cooking process is complete.

- Chiffonade – This is a slicing technique in which herbs or leafy green vegetables are cut into long, thin strips. It enables you to shred or finely cut produce.

- Chinois – A chinois is a conical strainer that helps you to remove impurities from a sauce. They are available for under £10 in most cookware shops. A chinois has an extremely fine mesh and so can strain purees, soups, sauces and custards to provide a fine texture.

- Drum Sieve – These wide, round, low-walled kitchen sieves can be used either to strain liquids or to sift and strain dry ingredients, including flour, powdered sugar and nuts. They are available in a variety of sizes.

- Julienne – Julienne, or French cut, is a culinary knife term to describe cutting ingredients into long, thin strips, similar to matchsticks.

- Mirepoix – A mirepoix is a selection of diced vegetables that are cooked for a long time on a gentle heat, without colouring or browning them. Frequently, a mirepoix will be made with butter or oil. It is not sautéed. Carrots, celery and onion make up the all-powerful culinary trio, which impart flavour and aroma to all types of dishes.

- Paco Jet – A Paco Jet is a kitchen appliance for professionals that micro-purees deep-frozen foods into ultra-fine textures without thawing. Typically, it will be used to make ice creams or sorbets. If you do not have one, use an ice cream churner as a substitute for your ice creams and sorbets.

- Parisienne Baller – This is a kitchen tool that allows you to cut small ball-shaped pieces from such fruit as melons or apples. The size is typically about 1cm to 3cm.

- Pastis – Hailing from France, Pastis is an anise-flavoured spirit with an abv of around 40-45%.

- Sosa Whip/Hy Foamer – Hy-foamer is a natural whipping agent used to improve or replace the use of egg whites. Hyfoamer will not over whisk or crack like an egg white will, it is also heat and acid stable which will allow for the production of flavoured meringues especially those with a strong citrus flavour and a low sugar content. Hy-foamer foams are light and compact, slightly more rigid than 'air' foams, will hold beautifully in a swipe or swirl and can be served warm or cold.

- Temperature Probe – A Digital Cooking Thermometer will ensure your food is cooked to perfection. It is especially good when cooking large joints of meat. The digital display will provide you with a very accurate and clear indication of the temperature in the centre of the food.

- Thermomix – The Thermomix is the world's most intelligent food processor. It lets you weigh, chop, blend, mix, grind, grate, cook, steam, whisk, knead and so much more all within one compact machine. A colour touchscreen beautifully displays digital recipes with guided cooking.

- Trimoline – Trimoline is an invert or inverted sugar, used widely in professional kitchens and bakeries. Trimoline helps to prevent crystallisation and gives a smoother texture in ice creams and ganaches. The thick colourless syrup also helps improve shelf life by preventing the absorption of moisture.

- Xanthan Gum – Xanthan Gum is for home baking with gluten free recipes to improve the crumb structure and to reduce crumbling. It is a polysaccharide with a wide variety of uses, including as a common food additive. It is a powerful thickening agent.

219

Index

A

Apples, Ormskirk Damson Sorbet with Granny Smith Apples & White Chocolate Soil 162, Granny Smith Apple and Calvados Sponge with Vanilla Mascarpone, Candied Walnuts 190

Asparagus, Confit Leg & Breast of Organic Rhug Estate Chicken & Claremont Farm Asparagus 86

B

Beef, A Plate of Callum's Oldfield Farm Galloway Beef to include Tongue, Cheek & Sirloin 90, Pave Rump of Salt Aged Lakeland Beef 182

Beetroot, Roast Breast of Squab Pigeon with Beetroot Puree & Foie Gras 186

Blackberries, Seared King Scallop with Butcher's Wife Black Pudding & Romanesco Cous Cous 168

Black Pudding, Warm Salad of Herdwick Lamb's Tongue, Butcher's Wife Black Pudding & Autumn Leaves 138, Seared King Scallop with Butcher's Wife Black Pudding & Romanesco Cous Cous 168, Senna Lane Farm Pork Belly, Cheek plus Southport smoked loin & Edges Butcher's Wife Black Pudding 174

Blood Orange, Fillet of Menai Mackerel, Blood Orange Dressing & Herb Infused Goats Curd 76

Bread, Glossary - Bread 204

Brown Shrimp, North Sea Haddock with Brown Shrimp & Herb Crust, Pickled Cucumber & Mustard 78, Cornish Red Mullet with Lemon, Parsley & Brown Shrimp Risotto and Pastis Sauce, 106

C

Cavolo Nero, Mr Ward's Loin of "Red Deer" Venison with Girolles, Black Truffle & Cavolo Nero 178

Caviar, Fillet of Turbot with Cucumber Tagliatelle, Palourde Clams, Cockles & Keta Caviar 144

Cherry, Baked Salsify, Parmesan Crust, Roast Navet & Sour Cherry Dressing 172

Chicken, Confit Leg & Breast of Organic Rhug Estate Chicken & Claremont Farm Asparagus 86

Chocolate, Valhrona Dark Chocolate Bordelou, Mango Foam, Matcha Green Tea Sorbet & Cremeux 94, Guanaja Dark Chocolate Mille Feuille 158, Sharing Plate, Includes: Pistachio Macaron, Chocolate Tart, Orange Delice & Choux Bun 192

Chouquette, Fresh Lime Tart with Earl Grey Sorbet and Caramel Chouquette 130

Choux Bun, Sharing Plate, Includes: Pistachio Macaron, Chocolate Tart, Orange Delice & Choux Bun 192

Clams, Fillet of Turbot with Cucumber Tagliatelle, Palourde Clams, Cockles & Keta Caviar 144, Liverpool Bay Seabass, Sauce of Palourde Clams, Celeriac Puree and Rainbow Chard 152

Coconut, Coconut Ice Cream, Chickpea Meringue, Rum Roasted Pineapple & Pineapple Gel 134

Cockles, Fillet of Turbot with Cucumber Tagliatelle, Palourde Clams, Cockles & Keta Caviar 144

Courgettes, Roast Courgettes with Curthwaite Goat's Curd & Tempura Courgette Flower 112

Courgette Flower, Roast Courgettes with Curthwaite Goat's Curd & Tempura Courgette Flower 112

Cous Cous, Seared King Scallop with Butcher's Wife Black Pudding & Romanesco Cous Cous 168

Crab, Pan-roast Fillet of Peterhead Hake with a Risotto of Filey Crab 156

Crème Brûlée, Crème Brûlée 100

Cucumber, North Sea Haddock with Brown Shrimp & Herb Crust, Pickled Cucumber & Mustard 78, Fillet of Cured Wild River Tweed Sea Trout, Sea Herbs, Samphire & Pickled Cucumber 110, Fillet of Turbot with Cucumber Tagliatelle, Palourde Clams, Cockles & Keta Caviar 144

D

Damson, Ormskirk Damson Sorbet with Granny Smith Apples & White Chocolate Soil 162

Duckling, Breast of Goosnargh Duckling with Rhubarb, Beetroot & Burnt Orange Purees 82

F

Fig, Warm Salad of Honey-glazed Roasted Fig, Spring Leaves & Tymsboro Goat's Cheese 74

Foie Gras, Roast Breast of Squab Pigeon with Beetroot Puree & Foie Gras 186

G

Girolles, Asian Marinated Tofu, Spaghetti Vegetables, Baby Spinach, Girolle Mushrooms & Pak Choi Shoots 124, Veal Cutlet, Shin and Marrow Bone with Girolles, Parsley Root & Heritage Carrots 150, Mr Ward's Loin of "Red Deer" Venison with Girolles, Black Truffle & Cavolo Nero 178

Goat's Cheese, Warm Salad of Honey-glazed Roasted Fig, Spring Leaves & Tymsboro Goat's Cheese 74

Goat's Curd, Fillet of Menai Mackerel, Blood Orange Dressing & Herb Infused Goats Curd 76, Roast Courgettes with Curthwaite Goat's Curd & Tempura Courgette Flower 112

Granola, The Captain's Trophy 96

H

Haddock, North Sea Haddock with Brown Shrimp & Herb Crust, Pickled Cucumber & Mustard 78

Hake, Pan-roast Fillet of Peterhead Hake, Pomme Mousseline & Southport Potted Shrimp 122, Pan-roast Fillet of Peterhead Hake with a Risotto of Filey Crab 156

Hogget, Summer Memories with Marjorie 114

Honey, Warm Salad of Honey-glazed Roasted Fig, Spring Leaves & Tymsboro Goat's Cheese 74

I

Ice Cream, The Captain's Trophy 96, Coconut Ice Cream, Chickpea Meringue, Rum Roasted Pineapple & Pineapple Gel 134, Pavlova of Gin-soaked Blackberries, Turkish Delight Ice Cream & White Chocolate Soil 164

J

Jus, Venison and damson jus 214, Natural Jus 215

L

Lamb's Tongue, Warm Salad of Herdwick Lamb's Tongue, Butcher's Wife Black Pudding & Autumn Leaves 138

Lancashire Cheese, Twice Baked Soufflé of Local Pink Tip Spinach & Mrs Kirkham's Lancashire Cheese 176

Leeks, Breast of Red Leg Partridge, Puy Lentils, Smoked Southport Pork Loin, Leeks & Pear 148

Lime Tart, Fresh Lime Tart with Earl Grey Sorbet and Caramel Chouquette 130

Lobster, Peterhead Turbot with Native Lobster, Lime and Mango salad and Mousseline potatoes 118

M

Macaron, Sharing Plate, Includes: Pistachio Macaron, Chocolate Tart, Orange Delice & Choux Bun 192

Mackerel, Fillet of Menai Mackerel, Blood Orange Dressing & Herb Infused Goats Curd 76

Mango, Valhrona Dark Chocolate Bordelou, Mango Foam, Matcha Green Tea Sorbet & Cremeux 94

Mascarpone, Granny Smith Apple and Calvados Sponge with Vanilla Mascarpone, Candied Walnuts 190

Meringue, The Captain's Trophy 96, Coconut Ice Cream, Chickpea Meringue, Rum Roasted Pineapple & Pineapple Gel 134, Pavlova of Gin-soaked Blackberries, Turkish Delight Ice Cream & White Chocolate Soil 164

Mousseline Potatoes, Peterhead Turbot with Native Lobster, Lime and Mango salad and Mousseline potatoes 118, Pan-roast Fillet of Peterhead Hake, Pomme Mousseline & Southport Potted Shrimp 122

Mullet, Cornish Red Mullet with Lemon, Parsley & Brown Shrimp Risotto and Pastis Sauce 106

Mustard, North Sea Haddock with Brown Shrimp & Herb Crust, Pickled Cucumber & Mustard 78

N

Navet, Baked Salsify, Parmesan Crust, Roast Navet & Sour Cherry Dressing 172

O

Orange, Breast of Goosnargh Duckling with Rhubarb, Beetroot & Burnt Orange Purees 82

P

Pak Choi, Asian Marinated Tofu, Spaghetti Vegetables, Baby Spinach, Girolle Mushrooms & Pak Choi Shoots 124

Parmesan, Baked Salsify, Parmesan Crust, Roast Navet & Sour Cherry Dressing 172

Partridge, Breast of Red Leg Partridge, Puy Lentils, Smoked Southport Pork Loin, Leeks & Pear 148

Passion Fruit, Passion Fruit Delice 128

Pear, Breast of Red Leg Partridge, Puy Lentils, Smoked Southport Pork Loin, Leeks & Pear 148

Pigeon, Roast Breast of Squab Pigeon with Beetroot Puree & Foie Gras 186

Pineapple, Coconut Ice Cream, Chickpea Meringue, Rum Roasted Pineapple & Pineapple Gel 134

Pistachio, Sharing Plate, Includes: Pistachio Macaron, Chocolate Tart, Orange Delice & Choux Bun 192

Pork, Breast of Red Leg Partridge, Puy Lentils, Smoked Southport Pork Loin, Leeks & Pear 148, Senna Lane Farm Pork Belly, Cheek plus Southport smoked loin & Edges Butcher's Wife Black Pudding 174

Potted Shrimp, Pan-roast Fillet of Peterhead Hake, Pomme Mousseline & Southport Potted Shrimp 122

Puree, Glossary - Puree (variety) 212

Puy Lentils, Breast of Red Leg Partridge, Puy Lentils, Smoked Southport Pork Loin, Leeks & Pear 148

R

Rabbit, Confit of Autumn Rabbit Pie with Pickled Vegetables & Piccalilli Vinaigrette 140

Rhubarb, Breast of Goosnargh Duckling with Rhubarb, Beetroot & Burnt Orange Purees 82

Risotto, Cornish Red Mullet with Lemon, Parsley & Brown Shrimp Risotto and Pastis Sauce 106, Pan-roast Fillet of Peterhead Hake with a Risotto of Filey Crab 156

S

Salad, Warm Salad of Honey-glazed Roasted Fig, Spring Leaves & Tymsboro Goat's Cheese 74, Warm Salad of Herdwick Lamb's Tongue, Butcher's Wife Black Pudding & Autumn Leaves 138

Salsify, Baked Salsify, Parmesan Crust, Roast Navet & Sour Cherry Dressing 172

Samphire, Fillet of Cured Wild River Tweed Sea Trout, Sea Herbs, Samphire & Pickled Cucumber 110

Seabass, Liverpool Bay Seabass, Sauce of Palourde Clams, Celeriac Puree and Rainbow Chard 152

Seasonings, Glossary - Seasonings (variety) 209

Sea Trout, Fillet of Cured Wild River Tweed Sea Trout, Sea Herbs, Samphire & Pickled Cucumber 110

Scallop, Seared King Scallop with Butcher's Wife Black Pudding & Romanesco Cous Cous 168

Sorbet, Valhrona Dark Chocolate Bordelou, Mango Foam, Matcha Green Tea Sorbet & Cremeux 94, Fresh Lime Tart with Earl Grey Sorbet and Caramel Chouquette 130, Ormskirk Damson Sorbet with Granny Smith Apples & White Chocolate Soil 162

Souffle, Twice Baked Soufflé of Local Pink Tip Spinach & Mrs Kirkham's Lancashire Cheese 176, Twice bake soufflé 214

Spinach, Asian Marinated Tofu, Spaghetti Vegetables, Baby Spinach, Girolle Mushrooms & Pak Choi Shoots 124, Twice Baked Soufflé of Local Pink Tip Spinach & Mrs Kirkham's Lancashire Cheese 176

Sponge, Granny Smith Apple and Calvados Sponge with Vanilla Mascarpone, Candied Walnuts 190

Stocks, Glossary - Stocks (variety) 206

Strawberries, The Captain's Trophy 96

T

Tofu, Asian Marinated Tofu, Spaghetti Vegetables, Baby Spinach, Girolle Mushrooms & Pak Choi Shoots 124

Truffle, Mr Ward's Loin of "Red Deer" Venison with Girolles, Black Truffle & Cavolo Nero 178

Turbot, Peterhead Turbot with Native Lobster, Lime and Mango salad and Mousseline potatoes 118, Fillet of Turbot with Cucumber Tagliatelle, Palourde Clams, Cockles & Keta Caviar 144

V

Veal, Veal Cutlet, Shin and Marrow Bone with Girolles, Parsley Root & Heritage Carrots 150

Venison, Mr Ward's Loin of "Red Deer" Venison with Girolles, Black Truffle & Cavolo Nero 178

W

Walnuts, Granny Smith Apple and Calvados Sponge with Vanilla Mascarpone, Candied Walnuts 190

White Chocolate, Crème Brûlée 100, Ormskirk Damson Sorbet with Granny Smith Apples & White Chocolate Soil 162, Pavlova of Gin-soaked Blackberries, Turkish Delight Ice Cream & White Chocolate Soil 164

Credits and Thank Yous

Thanks to all of my very special brigade at The Art School Restaurant for your support, handwork, dedication and encouragement in everything that we do, including producing this book.

A special mention to Vince for holding the fort on the recipe-writing days and Daniela for keeping me on track.

An enormous thanks too to our front-of-house team. Their work is vital in providing our guests with the welcome and hospitality that they would expect in our great city of Liverpool.

Thanks to Duncan at Relish Publications, Andy at A Way With Media, Michelle at Visual Voice Media and Paul at Media & You for their professionalism, tenacity and creative skills to get this book over the line.

Thanks to Victoria for test-driving the recipes and translating my chef-speak.

Thanks to Cathy for keeping me supplied in Jaffa Cakes, good humour and preserving my sanity.

Thanks to Matt at Pantone for his support, encouragement and for keeping things moving.

Thanks to our suppliers, a small yet distinguished list, who I am proud to work with and who who supply me with outstanding ingredients and who have become firm friends over the years.